MW00572850

Praise for *Hell (a guide)*

"They say the devil's greatest trick is convincing us that he doesn't exist. The same could be said for hell, which is most often seen today as a cartoonish land inhabited by comical figures with pitchforks and tails. But as Anthony DeStefano convincingly demonstrates in his page-turning new book, the reality of hell could not be more certain or more awful. Read this gripping and at times terrifying book to learn what Scripture says about hell—and discover the hope that exists for all to avoid it."

—ERIC METAXAS, *NEW YORK TIMES* BESTSELLING AUTHOR AND HOST OF THE NATIONALLY SYNDICATED *ERIC METAXAS RADIO SHOW*

"Powerful, inspirational, and frighteningly realistic, this book explains in the clearest terms possible what the Bible has to say about hell. A must-read for all Christians."

—MIKE HUCKABEE, FORMER GOVERNOR OF ARKANSAS AND HOST OF *HUCKABEE*

"Certainly the best book on hell ever written. Profound, provocative, and deeply sobering, this remarkable book will help anyone who has ever wondered if hell is real. For Heaven's sake—read it!"

—DR. DICK EASTMAN, INTERNATIONAL PRESIDENT OF EVERY HOME FOR CHRIST AND FOUNDING MEMBER AND PRESIDENT OF AMERICA'S NATIONAL PRAYER COMMITTEE

hell

Also by Anthony DeStefano

hell

(a guide)

Anthony DeStefano

NELSON
BOOKS

An Imprint of Thomas Nelson

Published in Nashville, Tennessee, by Nelson Books, an imprint of Thomas Nelson. Nelson Books and Thomas Nelson are registered trademarks of HarperCollins Christian Publishing, Inc.

Thomas Nelson titles may be purchased in bulk for educational, business, fund-raising, or sales promotional use. For information, please e-mail SpecialMarkets@ThomasNelson.com.

Unless otherwise noted, Scripture quotations are taken from the Holy Bible, New International Version®, NIV®. Copyright © 1973, 1978, 1984, 2011 by Biblica, Inc.® Used by permission of Zondervan. All rights reserved worldwide. www.zondervan.com. The "NIV" and "New International Version" are trademarks registered in the United States Patent and Trademark Office by Biblica, Inc.®

Scripture quotations marked KJV are from the King James Version. Public domain.

Scripture quotations marked ESV are from the ESV® Bible (The Holy Bible, English Standard Version®), copyright © 2001 by Crossway, a publishing ministry of Good News Publishers. Used by permission. All rights reserved.

Scripture quotations marked NASB are from New American Standard Bible®, Copyright © 1960, 1962, 1963, 1968, 1971, 1972, 1973, 1975, 1977, 1995 by The Lockman Foundation. Used by permission. (www.Lockman.org)

Any internet addresses, phone numbers, or company or product information printed in this book are offered as a resource and are not intended in any way to be or to imply an endorsement by Thomas Nelson, nor does Thomas Nelson vouch for the existence, content, or services of these sites, phone numbers, companies, or products beyond the life of this book.

ISBN 978-0-7180-8062-4 (eBook)
ISBN 978-0-7180-8061-7 (HC)

Library of Congress Control Number: 2020934937

Printed in the United States of America

20 21 22 23 24 LSC 10 9 8 7 6 5 4 3 2 1

This book is dedicated to all victims
of evil everywhere.

Abandon Hope, All Ye Who Enter Here*

Midway through the journey of our life, I found myself within a dark wood, for I had wandered off the straight path. . . . How I entered there I cannot say. . . . But when I reached the foot of a hill that rose up at the end of the valley, my heart plunged in deep fear. . . . A figure presented itself to my eyes. . . . "You will have to go by another road," he said to me. . . . "If you want to escape this wilderness . . . I will be your guide and lead you from here to an eternal place, where you will listen to cries of despair and see ancient tormented spirits who lament forever their second death." . . . And I said to him: "Poet, I implore you . . . help me escape this evil. . . . Lead me to the place you speak of so I may . . . see those whom you say are full of sorrow." Then he set out, and I kept close behind him.

—FROM THE OPENING CANTO OF DANTE'S
INFERNO (AUTHOR'S TRANSLATION)

---

* The inscription over the entrance gate to hell (Dante Alighieri, *The Inferno*, Canto 3).

Contents

An Infernal Itinerary

Why Would Anyone Want a Guide to Hell?

There are so many guides on the market today. Guides to romantic destinations, historic destinations, luxury destinations, religious destinations, culturally significant destinations, even poverty-stricken destinations. These guides vary greatly in nature and style depending on their subject matter, but they all have one thing in common: they all presume that people *want* to go to the places they describe.

This guide is different. It's about a place no one wants to go or, more precisely, a place no one *says* they want to go or *thinks* they want to go. Yet if you believe the Bible, the world's major religions, and the greatest saints and spiritual leaders who have ever lived, people end up going there all the time.

Of course, we're talking about hell. The Bible uses various Hebrew and Greek words that we translate as *hell*. These include *hades*, *tartarus*, and *sheol*, each of which has a different meaning. But the hell we are interested in is the place Christ referred to as *Gehenna*, that abominable "lake of fire" and "second death" reserved for the damned, that place of eternal pain, punishment, "gnashing of teeth," and sorrow.[1]

Christ spoke about hell eleven times in the Gospels, and he described it in the strongest possible terms.[2] He made it clear that hell exists, not figuratively, not metaphorically, not mythologically, but literally. There are souls of human beings there right now, as you read these words. And someday, after what Christians call the "resurrection of the dead," more people will be in hell, not just spiritually, but in bodily form as well.[3]

Now why would anyone want a guide to somewhere so unpleasant? Because no matter how much traveling you do in life, there are only two destinations that ultimately matter—heaven or hell. And that's why I've written this book, because we have to *begin* in hell if we want to avoid *ending up* there.

Many other authors have attempted to write about this subject, most notably Dante Alighieri in *The Inferno*, John Milton in *Paradise Lost*, and C. S. Lewis in *The Great Divorce* and *The Screwtape Letters*. While my guide is not to be compared to those masterpieces, it does have one advantage: those other books are either epic poems or works of fiction, and as such they depict hell in symbolic and allegorical terms. The whole purpose of this book is to show you what hell is *actually* like. To show you hell up close and personal. To give you all the distressing details. To keep things theologically correct but as simple, straightforward, and *real* as possible.

Like all guidebooks, this one attempts to describe the sights, sounds, and sensations of its destination. It discusses the historical background and explores local customs, laws, and governing structures. It talks about the kinds of individuals you might meet and describes the accommodations that might be provided for the inhabitants, as well as the activities available to them.

This guide is essentially designed to allow you to visit the bottom of the bottomless pit without having to descend one step, to see the infamous fire and brimstone without having to get burned, to take a grand tour of all the hellish tortures you've heard about without having to experience them firsthand, and—one hopes—without enduring an overly preachy, difficult text.

Be advised, however, that travelers making this excursion today should take a few precautions. First, no matter your spiritual beliefs, an open mind is necessary. For the moment we haven't even defined what hell is or speculated where it might be located or given any particulars of what it might be like, other than to assert that it exists.

Second, it's important to understand our limited scope. This is not a book of Christian apologetics. It is not designed to demonstrate God's existence or prove any specific doctrine of faith. Rather, it assumes a basic belief in God and presents an orthodox interpretation of the Christian teaching on hell, a teaching that most traditions within Christianity will have no trouble accepting.

Third, because of this limited scope, we will not be discussing subjects such as purgatory. Purgatory is a Catholic belief stating that, since we must be in perfect agreement with the Father's will in order to enter heaven, there is a process of purification that saved souls must endure before seeing God face-to-face. It is not the purpose of this book to explain this doctrine—a source of significant contention between Catholics and Protestants for hundreds of years. Nor are we particularly concerned with presenting any rigorous moral or dogmatic theology. Indeed, there

XVI | An Infernal Itinerary

are many topics we could explore in a bigger book—for example, the meaning and nature of baptism and the age-old controversy between the importance of faith and works. But this is not a book on how to lead a good Christian life or even what it means to be saved. It's about one thing: what hell is like. And we will consider theological doctrines only as they make hell understandable and believable.

Believability is fundamental to this guide. That's why there is a fourth point to keep in mind. Before going any further, you should be prepared to engage in some honest self-reflection. So many people—even good Christians—have a problem accepting that an all-good, loving, and merciful God could create such a hideous place as hell and that he could force people he supposedly loves to suffer there forever. They can't wrap their minds around the idea of a God who sentences anyone to eternal punishment.

This thinking, though understandable, is based on a faulty interpretation of the Christian concept of hell and the nature of evil. For evil is really the key to this whole book. It's the key to unlocking the mystery of eternal punishment in hell. As we shall see, once you understand how it's possible to love evil, it will be much easier to understand how some people can desire to be in hell, how they can actually want to be punished forever. Therefore it is essential we embark on a study of what it means to be evil.

Unfortunately there is only one way to do that. To really grasp the meaning of hell requires that you first humble yourself and search the innermost core of your being to discover *your own capacity for evil.* You must dig and probe deeply, despite any unpleasant things you might find. Essentially you have to go down before you can go up. You have to pass through the darkness of your own soul in order to understand the darkness of hell. Only in this way can you finally come back out into the light.

This involves radical self-honesty, which can be extremely uncomfortable and even painful. And yet it is absolutely necessary in order to comprehend the torments of hell in all their vivid reality and understand the kind of people who experience them.

If all of this makes sense, then we're ready to begin our trip.

The Starting Point
of Our Trip

The Enemy Within

All journeys, no matter their final destination, have a starting point. And that starting point is usually home.

The journey we are going to make is no different. Before we visit hell—before we define what it is, speak about its history and significance, and explore who goes there and what it's like to be there—we have to do something else. We have to get into the proper mind-set. We have to choose a point of origin. We cannot start a tour of hell *in* hell itself. We must start elsewhere. And the only logical starting place is home—that is, the state of *our own souls*.

The reason we can't begin with hell is because people's opinions of what it might be like vary too much. At one end of the spectrum are those who think hell is complete nonsense, a product of religious and psychological superstition, a fictitious punishment the Christian church has used to beat people into submission for thousands of years. On the other end of the spectrum are those who believe in a ridiculously cartoonish version of hell, complete with a red devil with horns and a pitchfork and steamy black smoke coming out of his ears.

Then there are those who believe that hell is a myth, a product of evolutionary thought that has great value, at least in terms of understanding human history and psychology. However, they don't think this myth has any real basis in fact. On the other hand, some people believe hell is real, but only as a potential reality, and that no one actually goes there because of a doctrine known as universal salvation, which states that, in the end, God finds a way to allow everyone to go to heaven, no matter what they've done in life.

Finally, there are those who believe hell does indeed have mythological and psychological meaning, but that it also exists in reality as a place or state of eternal suffering, both in a spiritual way now and later on, after the resurrection of the dead, in a physical way, and that people do indeed go there. This is the position considered to be the most traditional and orthodox in Christian theology, and it is the position of this book.

But we can't start there. There's just too much disagreement. We have to get there first. And the best way to do that is to start with something that nobody with common sense has any doubts about: the connection between hell and evil.

No matter what your belief regarding the definition of hell, everyone agrees that the concept of hell—true or not—has something to do with the concept of evil, evil people, and the final destination of evil people. Whether or not that destination is a real place or a psychological state or a state of annihilation or a literary device is something we haven't gotten to yet. But we at least know the idea of hell has to do with the idea of where evil people might end up. On this point there is a general consensus.

Now if the trajectory of evil is hell, then the starting point of any travel guide to hell must be the evil we already know—namely, the evil that exists in the world right now.

What exactly is evil? That can be a complicated question too. Some atheist philosophies deny the existence of evil or at least say it's necessary for humans to go "beyond good and evil" in order to live authentic lives. But we are going to ignore these philosophies for now. First, because we can't get bogged down in absurdity. Second, because some of the very same atheists who deny the existence of evil are also the ones who have perpetrated the greatest acts of evil in the history of the world: Stalin, Hitler, Mao Zedong, and Pol Pot, to name a few.

Besides those who deny evil on philosophical grounds, there has also been a pernicious movement underway since the time of Sigmund Freud and the birth of psychoanalysis to categorize all evil as mental illness. According to this way of thinking, Hitler, Stalin, and the other murderers, rapists, and child abusers of history weren't evil; they simply had severe psychopathic and antisocial personality disorders.

That's not the Christian understanding of evil or psychology. Yes, it's possible for someone to be a true psychopath, possessing a chronic mental disorder that results in criminal behavior, but that's not the whole story. Christianity has always believed that evil is a reality—both personal and cosmic—and that it has to do with evil choices that are freely made. Many modern psychologists deny the existence of free will to begin with, so of course they must also deny the existence of evil and instead attribute all malevolent behavior to genetics or developmental problems in childhood or adolescence.

But again, we are not going to entertain such nonsense. For the purpose of this discussion we are going to accept what the great masses of humanity have always known: evil exists and is all around us, even inside us, and there are no words to adequately describe how unbelievably vicious, violent, twisted, and abominable it can be.

A quick review of just a few gruesome details associated with human activity throughout history is sufficient to establish this reality. We could go all the way back to the biblical story of Cain and Abel and the first murder.[1] We could talk about the ritualistic sacrifice of children in ancient Carthage. We could describe all the nightmarish tortures long ago invented to inflict excruciating pain on human beings, from crucifixion to the medieval rack and saw to the practice of boiling people in oil.

But we don't have to confine ourselves to the ancient world. The most monstrous evil has taken place in recent, more "civilized" times. Between 1900 and 2020, more than 150 million people were brutally butchered by totalitarian dictators and their regimes.[2] The twentieth century saw a plethora of merciless wars caused by these evil governments, as well as mass executions, forced starvations, gulags, concentration camps, gas chambers, and unspeakable experiments on children.

The twenty-first century hasn't been much better. Think of September 11 and other acts of terrorism perpetrated against the innocent. Think of the mass shootings at schools or the thousands of serial rapes and murders that take place every year in every corner of the globe. Think of the whole culture of death, with abortion and infanticide and forced euthanasia becoming inscribed in law in every part of the world. Think of the random, disconnected acts of unprovoked cruelty we see in the news all the time: the woman who poured gasoline on her sleeping children and burned them alive; the man who kidnapped a teenage girl, repeatedly raped her, stabbed her, and put salt into her wounds before finally dismembering her. There's just no end to the atrocities.

The horror is not only that people are being abused; it's the unmitigated malice and barbarism behind the abuse. It's not just that people are killing other people; it's the heinousness of the murders themselves, the desire of the killers to humiliate, torment, and inflict misery on their victims. It's not just the blood; it's the bloodthirstiness, the sheer sadism, and the wickedness of it all. Yes, *wickedness*.

We're not talking here about crimes of passion. Nor are we talking about crimes committed purely for ambition's sake. We're talking about crimes in which the perpetrators seem to take *joy* in bestowing suffering on others. We're talking about cold, premeditated, methodical savagery.

This is the face of evil. And there is something definitely diabolical about it, something otherworldly, something disconnected from abnormal psychology or the politics of power or any naturalistic principle concerning the so-called survival of the fittest. It's a phenomenon that stands completely apart from the realm of atoms and molecules and the material universe. It just doesn't make sense in rational terms. And this *spiritual* quality of evil is impossible to deny. Examples of it are too numerous and too startling and too twisted. The fact is that while evil is not more powerful than good, it is certainly more visible. In fact, evil is the most visible of all the invisible realities proclaimed by the religions of the world.

That is why evil, ironically, can often be the gateway to deeper faith and spirituality for those who are naturally inclined to skepticism. Despite the denial of metaphysical evil by most modern philosophers and psychologists, many people who have difficulty believing in invisible, spiritual realities are sometimes led to a belief in the supernatural through the undeniable *experience* of evil. To paraphrase G. K. Chesterton, the existence of evil is the only religious doctrine that can really be empirically proven. That's why some people come to believe in the devil *before* they believe in God.

But we'll talk more about that paradox later. At this point we're still discussing the existence of evil and its seeming pervasiveness. And we have to go further still. If we want to understand anything about hell, we can't just do a survey of the evil monsters of history and leave it at that for the simple reason that it's too easy to dismiss them as monsters. It's too easy to class them as aberrations and exceptions to the general goodness of humanity. If we want to go deeper into the subject of evil, we have to look at the evil inside ourselves.[3]

And here is where things get a little difficult. None of us ever likes to admit that we are capable of doing truly evil things. Yes, we acknowledge the fact that we sometimes fall short of the mark, that we occasionally do bad things, and even that much of the time we can be pretty consistent sinners, however we define sin. But that's quite different from being a Hitler or a terrorist or a cold-blooded killer. *Those* are the people we associate with evil, the monsters of the world. And since we obviously don't put ourselves into the monster category, most of us don't consider ourselves evil.

But that's only partly true. That kind of thinking misses the point because it doesn't go far enough. It's too shallow. It's too dishonest. It's not self-reflective enough. It only considers our actions from the point of view of our present circumstances. It doesn't address the free choices we are actually making in the center of our wills. It doesn't delve deeply enough into our dark sides. It doesn't ask the question: What if things were different in my life—how would I act? It therefore doesn't address our personal *capacity* for evil.

That's what we need to examine. What are we doing inside our heads from moment to moment? What kind of dark, secret thoughts are we harboring that we wouldn't dream of telling anyone? Most important, if these secret thoughts had something more substantial backing them up, what would our behavior look like?

You see, right now, most of you reading this book are very limited in your ability to act out your evil inclinations. Not only do you lack sufficient money and power, but you also lack sufficient motivation. You're sitting in a warm room with a roof over your head, the lights are on, and you have food in your stomach. Even though you may have a lot of problems to deal with, you're not starving. Compared to other people in the world, you're doing okay. But what if you found yourself in totally different circumstances? What if your whole life fell apart? What if you and those you loved really were struggling to eat and drink and survive? What would you do then?

Or, contrarily, what if your position was much stronger than it is now? What if you had unlimited power and wealth and the ability to satisfy your every little desire, just like the twentieth-century totalitarian leaders who caused so much carnage? How would you behave?

Please don't misunderstand me. I'm not accusing you of being a monster. Nor am I denying the existence of free will and the ability of human beings to triumph over their circumstances. I'm not saying the only difference between the average person on the street and Adolf Hitler is that Hitler had an army of brutal Nazis behind him. I'm not claiming everyone is as bad as Hitler or that everything you do in life comes down to your upbringing and environment. If Hitler had been born into a different family in a different country in a different century, I don't think he would have been a much different person, at least not in terms of his will to choose evil. I don't believe he would have been a wonderfully warm, loving, and kindhearted individual. No. His evil inclinations would have manifested themselves in other ways and other actions. In his soul, he would still have made dark, selfish, evil choices. He just wouldn't have been in a position to murder six million Jews and set a whole world aflame. The scope of his evil would have been greatly restricted.

The point is that while we don't want to overemphasize the importance of environment so much that we deny the existence of evil, we also don't want to lose sight of the fact that circumstantial factors do have the ability to *hide* evil. That's the crux of the matter. There are a lot more evil people out there than we commonly imagine. We just don't see them. They don't have the power, the money, the courage, or the fame to carry out their evil impulses. Much of their evil has never been brought to the surface. It's been rendered relatively harmless because of their situation in life.

And that's exactly what you have to realize about yourself too. Not that you are evil through and through. But that there may be a great deal more evil inside you than you are aware of. There may be a great deal more evil that you are capable of if you had been born into a different situation, if you had the means, motive, and opportunity to do what you truly wanted.

Before we embark on this trip to hell, it is absolutely imperative that you consider this fact. This is not meant to be an exercise in self-flagellation; rather, it's meant to enable you to really understand why hell exists in the first place and why people actually want to go there. (Yes, I said *want* to go there).

For just a few minutes, focus on your inner capacity for evil. Don't try to deny it or minimize it or rationalize it or even judge it. Just look at it. Turn it around in your mind. Think about the most vile things you have ever done or said or thought. Think about your outbursts of prideful anger, your lapses into sexual sins, perhaps your drinking binges, your bouts of gluttony, your lying, your laziness, your cowardice, your ungratefulness, or your selfishness. Think about how many times you have indulged in this kind of behavior. Think about the times you have reveled in it. Think about how many times you have resolved to do better or to change and yet, the second you encountered even the tiniest temptation, you slithered right back into the mud.

And then, once you've called all that to mind, realize that these aren't even the worst sins you've committed. In fact, many of the things I just listed—though outwardly repugnant because of the damage they cause—often have a minimal amount of personal culpability attached to them. In other words, they're not completely your fault. They're at least partially brought on by emotion or fatigue or hunger or suffering or habit or mental illness or insecurity or addictive inclinations or natural inclinations. Thus, the degree to which God holds you accountable for them (according to Christian teaching) may be significantly mitigated, because they are not truly *free* choices of the will.

No, what I'm talking about now are the other bad things you do, the sins that are really serious. The ones you keep totally hidden and don't even like to admit to yourself. The ones you commit in a calm, cold, and almost detached state of mind.

I'm talking about those times when you inwardly take pleasure in other people's failings or tragedies. Maybe even those of your family and friends.

I'm talking about the times you betray someone's trust. It doesn't matter if the circumstances seem insignificant and the consequences minimal. No act of betrayal is small.

I'm talking about lying or gossiping about people for the express purpose of denigrating them. Or knowingly trying to drag them down because they're happy about something and you secretly resent them for it. I'm talking about purposely hurting someone you're supposed to love.

I'm talking about all the times you closely monitor and calculate your words, not because you care so much about their substance but because you so desperately want to be perceived as smart or good or rich or important. I'm talking about all the communication you do that is insincere and even hypocritical. I'm talking about that lust for status and significance that pervades so much of your interior life: the underlying jealousy, envy, arrogance, and self-centeredness that lies behind so many of your thoughts and actions.

But there's more. The worst kinds of sins are those in which you persist in evil behavior no matter what the consequences and no matter what suffering you cause or what pain you have to endure yourself. For example, have you ever purposely tried to cultivate emotions of resentment in order to whip yourself up into a frenzy of self-righteous indignation? Have you ever willfully chosen to stew in bitterness and bile because it felt good, so good in fact that you wanted to be that way rather than to be cheerful and lighthearted and happy? Have you ever shaken your fist in outrage at the world or wallowed in self-pity rather than take a few simple actions that might put you into a more pleasant state of mind?

Have there ever been times in your life when you were *not* driven by compulsion or habit and yet still did something you *knew* violated your conscience, despite any risk of consequences, because you just didn't care? Have you ever dug your heels in and refused to either apologize for something you did wrong or to accept someone else's apology, even though you were well aware that your refusal was harming relationships with family members or friends?

These are the kinds of prideful and hypocritical sins that Christ condemned so vehemently, much more vehemently than he ever condemned any sins of the flesh.[4] These are the sins of the will. And my friend, you know you're guilty of some of them! You know that some of the secret things that go on inside your head are absolutely toxic!

But it's not just you. It's me too! It's humanity in general. We all make these kinds of hellish choices from time to time. We all choose to do things we know are evil, persist in that evil, and then refuse to be sorry for that evil, even when it leads to pain and suffering. Sometimes it's just more pleasurable for us to suffer in pride than to repent and reverse course in humility.

To admit this is not to indulge in self-loathing or self-defeating guilt. It's to be honest. It's to gain a better understanding of evil, a better understanding of Hitler and Stalin and all the terrorists and serial killers we referred to earlier. The point is not to equate ourselves with Nazis but to realize that, to some degree, deep inside each of us exists the same ugliness and darkness of spirit that motivated the Nazis. It's a spirit that doesn't care one iota about authentic authority or morality or consequences or punishments. It's a spirit that only cares about the satisfaction of pride and willful selfishness. It's a spirit that, sufficiently developed, might actually *prefer* punishment to paradise, hell to heaven.

The bottom line is that, to understand the evil monsters who inhabit the bowels of hell, you must first get in touch with the evil monsters who live inside your soul. That's the mind-set you have to have in order for this guidebook to mean anything. That's the starting point for any authentic tour of the underworld.

If you're strong enough and honest enough to do that, then we're ready to take the second step in our journey. We're ready to learn something about the history of hell. After all, how exactly did this place or state first come into being? What are its origins? It's time to relate what can only be described as the strangest story in the world. A tale that, if true, is more frightening than any horror movie ever dreamed up in Hollywood.

It's the story of the fall of the demons.

The Origin of Hell

The Story of the Demons

Let's review the few small steps we've taken so far on this journey to hell.

First, we made the simple observation that hell has to do with the idea of evil and where evil people end up. Second, we gave some examples of the evil around us and inside us. Third, we said we need to keep these examples at the front of our minds for the time being because they are going to help us to better understand why there is a hell, what hell is like, and who goes there.

The next step is to discuss hell itself, its origin and history, and the fact that it is everlasting.

This last point is really the key. I think most people who

believe in God wouldn't have so much of a problem accepting the idea of hell if it weren't for the fact that it is supposed to last forever. Once you embrace the notion of a personal deity, the proposition that there might be some form of punishment for violating that deity's commandments or standards of morality is not unreasonable. Indeed, it's a concept that most of us probably welcome. After all, most of us have encountered injustice in our lives. Most of us have witnessed or heard about cases of evil that have gone unpunished. "Life is so unfair" is such a common refrain. Therefore, the idea that somewhere, somehow justice might be carried out by an almighty, all-knowing, all-good God is not at all unpleasant. The scales of justice have to be balanced at some point, otherwise life would be absurd.

But it is the *eternal* nature of this punishment that is so difficult for us to come to grips with. That just doesn't seem right to most people. In fact, it seems cruel. Life on earth is so short. It goes by in the blink of an eye. How can any crime, no matter how great, deserve an eternity of torment? If time in hell is measured in years (and we'll get to that question later on), then God might conceivably sentence a serial killer to several centuries or even several millennia of prison in hell. But forever? The killer's crime, no matter how grievous, is finite, after all. How could his punishment be infinite?

And even if hell were not a punishment in the sense that word is usually understood, but rather some kind of free choice made by evil people to go there, why would it have to be a permanent choice? Why couldn't the souls who inhabit hell change their minds after a period of time and repent of their sins or do whatever God wants them to do in order to leave that terrible place?

It may seem as if we are putting the cart before the horse by discussing the question of eternity* before we clarify what we mean by hell, but it's actually the best way to proceed on this tour. So many people either disbelieve in hell or don't take it seriously because they get stuck here, at the idea that it never ends. We have to get over this hurdle before we can go any further.

Perhaps the easiest way of doing that is to tell the story of the origin of hell. After all, guidebooks always include a short section on the history of the place they're trying to describe. This guidebook is no different. We said in the last chapter that there is a whole range of theories about what hell really is. For the moment, let's put aside all symbolic, psychological, metaphorical, and mythological definitions. We can always draw out these deeper implications later. For now, let's present the story of hell as Christianity teaches it, in its literal sense.

What follows is a rough sketch, but it is accurate from a theological point of view. Its purpose is not to prove the existence of hell but to show that, if you accept the story as true, it makes sense that hell lasts forever.

And it is a strange story indeed.

It all starts with the fact that God is a *creator*. He loves to make things. If you believe God exists, then all you have to do is look around at the world to see the truth of this statement: the planets, the stars, the earth with its oceans and mountains and valleys and deserts and glorious colors and millions of different life forms. God's superabundant desire to create is simply self-evident.[1]

Moreover, this divine desire does not extend only to the

---

* Eternity is used here in a generic sense to indicate endlessness rather than an existence that has no beginning.

visible cosmos. God has created a whole invisible world as well, full of invisible creatures called angels. Everyone knows angels play an important role in the Christian religion as well as in Judaism and Islam. But Christianity in particular has a significant number of clear teachings about these wondrous and enigmatic beings.

It teaches, for example, that God created the angels in the same way he created the universe and human beings—namely, out of nothing. It teaches that, like human beings, angels have an intellect and free will. It teaches that angels have spectacular powers that are cosmic in magnitude. It teaches that the number of angels is prodigious, using words such as *armies*, *legions*, and *multitudes* to describe them.[2]

It teaches that there seems to be, within these multitudes, a mysterious hierarchy or system of ranking.[3] Finally, it teaches that the main thing that distinguishes angels from the rest of creation is that they are *pure spirits*.[4]

As I discussed in my book *Angels All Around Us*, the concept of a pure spirit is something very alien to us. The only reality we know is spatial and temporal. It's almost impossible for us to imagine anything else. To be a pure spirit means that you're alive in some way but that you don't have a body. It means you're not visible to the eye. It means you're not bound by any of the limits that time and space and matter impose upon human beings.

What are these limits?

Well, material objects and living creatures have to be in one place at one time and can only get to another place if they physically move there inch by inch, foot by foot, mile by mile. This depends on the process of locomotion. In fact, every function performed by living creatures is dependent upon their physical design, their construction, and some kind of regulating process. The way we get our energy, the way we dispose of waste, the way we come to know things. All this is tied in some way or another to our bodies. Even the way we think and feel is wired through our nervous systems and our brains. The most significant limitation of any living creature (or inanimate mechanism for that matter) is that it deteriorates over time. It ages. It gets old and worn and loses its ability to function and eventually dies.

To be a pure spirit, according to Christian teaching, means you have none of these limitations. It means you're not bound by the constraints of physical space. You don't have to move in order to go somewhere. You can just be there whenever your will commands it. It means you don't have to think with the help of bodily organs like a brain; you don't have to depend on your senses to learn things, see things, smell things, or hear things. And it means you don't ever deteriorate. To be a pure spirit means, by definition, that you are immortal.[5]

Now we mentioned that angels have their own intellect and free will. What that means is they have the ability to think for themselves and choose for themselves. But since angels are pure spirits, their intellect works much differently than ours for the simple reason that they don't have material bodies and neurological systems through which ideas have to be filtered. They just see and know ideas intuitively and then freely make decisions about them. For instance, when they were created, they had the power to choose between right and wrong, to serve God or work against him, to obey him or disobey him, just as human beings do today. But they didn't have to process these ideas with a neurological system before acting. They were able to immediately grasp the ideas and choices put before them and then decide on them.

And this is where the story of the angels gets so interesting. Angels are much more powerful than human beings. Their intellects are stronger. Their wills are stronger. And according to the Bible, they have the ability to profoundly affect the material world with these intellects and wills. In fact, according to the Bible, they have the power to destroy whole cities, to bring down pestilence and fire upon the earth, and to wreak much more havoc through their evil choices than we ever could.[6] That's why it's eerie and intriguing to read in Scripture that soon after the creation of the angels, a war broke out among them.[7]

What seems to have happened was that sometime after they were created by God, one of them made a remarkable and surprising choice. God had given him the power to exercise his will freely, and that's exactly what he did. Only he didn't choose to thank God for making him or to praise him or worship him or follow him, as the other angels did. On the contrary, this angel made a clear decision to follow his own will, to choose against God's will, to *reject* God.

This angel has been called by a variety of names: Lucifer, Satan, and the devil. He seems to have been extremely powerful. He seems to have had a very high rank in the hierarchy of angels. Indeed, this angel seems to have been the brightest and most brilliant of all angels. In fact, one of his names means Morning Star.[8] Anyway, this special angel proceeded to launch an all-out rebellion against God. He even succeeded in persuading whole legions of angels to join with him in his terrible cause.

Why did he launch this rebellion?

No one knows for sure. Certainly, we can see in our own lives that it's possible to reject God's will, to hate God's will, and even to fight against God's will. And if it's possible for weak human beings to choose to battle God, it's certainly possible for Satan and the angels, who are so much more powerful.

According to the Scriptures, the primary cause of the satanic rebellion was pride. "I will raise my throne above the stars of God," he said. "I will make myself like the Most High."[9] At the core of Satan's rebellion was his desire to assert his radical independence from God as well as his desire to be Godlike in terms of raw power. And this was due to his great self-love and the resentment and hatred of God born of that self-love.

Satan then communicated his choice to the other angels. But remember, because angels are pure spirits, they communicate differently than we do. They don't speak with sounds. They don't express their thoughts in words. They don't have mouths and tongues and voice boxes. They don't have any of those means of communication at their disposal. But what they have is something better, something faster: they are able to instantaneously convey the essence of their thoughts to one another through some kind of direct mind-to-mind contact.

This is really what Scripture means by saying there was a war in heaven. A war is defined as a state of hostile conflict between nations that usually results in a great loss of life and much suffering. And that's exactly what happened. Angels are pure spirits, so any battles they have between each other must primarily be battles of intellect and will. Their weapons are essentially arguments. When Satan communicated his rebellious decision to the other angels, he gave them his reason too. Most of them did not agree with him. Most were grateful to God and loved their Creator. One of these faithful angels has been singled out in Scripture as being particularly close to God—namely, the archangel Michael.[10] But a good portion of the angels made the same choice as Satan.[11] A good portion were blinded by their own greatness. They overrated their abilities and powers to such a degree that they totally disregarded God's supremacy and refused to take part in his plan for creation. The whole story of the demons, in fact, can be summed up in the infamous phrase often attributed to Satan: *Non serviam* ("I will not serve").

It's critical to understand that the devil and the angels who followed him understood the situation clearly; they knew who God was and knew they owed their existence to him. And yet they still made a conscious, purposeful, and free choice to reject him.

Follow this closely now! Because angels are pure spirits, their decision was one of pure spiritual pride, not influenced in any way by environment or circumstances or physical imperfections or upbringing or genetics or biases or passions or incomplete information. Because they are pure spirits, *their choice was irrevocable.*

And here we come to the main point of this chapter: the *fixed* nature of angelic decisions. Angels don't have bodies. They don't have neurological systems. They don't have to process their thoughts through neurons and synapses and brain cells. We can't relate to this in the slightest, because all human beings ever do is process ideas. All we ever do is make choices based on how and when we filter a thousand different variables through the prism of our material bodies. It takes time for us to see something, then for our brains to recognize what we see, then to compare it to everything else we've ever seen, to analyze it, measure it, weigh it, and finally to make a decision about it. Even the simplest act of recognizing a friend or family member involves a process like this. We're able to do it very quickly, of course, but it's not instantaneous. Our brain still has to go through many unseen steps.

It's this succession of mental steps that results in the possibility of error. There's always a chance we might get our facts wrong, or that we might not get all the information we need, or that we might get the information at the wrong time. There's a chance we might be too tired to process everything correctly or that our emotions or our lack of intelligence or our environment or our natural biases might, in some way, cause us to make the wrong decision. There are a million different reasons why it's possible to make a mistake. That's why we're constantly changing our minds. That's why we're always going back and forth, round and round in circles, without ever coming to a decision we're really sure about. Ultimately, that's why we're able to recognize our errors and be *sorry* for them.

It's not like that for the angels. As pure spirits they don't have to process their thoughts as we do. They immediately see whatever they're looking at from every angle. They don't have to wait for more information. They don't have to conduct any research. They don't have to try to figure out a problem. They don't ever have to sleep on it. Nor do they ever worry they made a mistake, because there's never any deliberation involved. There's never any anxiety that they missed something. They already fully possess all the facts from the moment they identify the thing they have to decide about. They grasp everything instantaneously. All angels really have to do is see something and choose. And once they make that choice, it's forever, because they have made their choice with complete conviction and in full possession of all possible data.

I know it's difficult to get our minds around this, but once we do, we won't ever have trouble understanding the process by which angels make decisions or the concept that their decisions are irrevocable.

And this concept isn't as alien as it might at first seem. You've made choices like this, too, though you may not realize it, because they don't even seem like choices. Just think of something you're completely sure of. Something you're so certain of that you'd bet your life on it. It doesn't have to be something big. It can be something small. I mentioned before the experience of recognizing a family member. Well, right now, as I am writing these words, my wife is bringing me a cup of coffee. I'm looking at her face as I type. She's raising her eyebrow, wondering why I'm staring at her with such a blank expression (the expression I usually have when I'm thinking). The point is this: I'm absolutely positive it's my wife I'm looking at. It's not my brother. It's not my sister. It's not my mother-in-law. It's not some stranger. Why am I so sure? Because I have all the facts at my fingertips. Because my eyes have been checked and I have perfect vision. Because I've known my wife for decades. In the act of recognizing her—that is, distinguishing her from other people—I've made a decision. It's not a big decision and it's not a moral decision, but it's a decision nonetheless. And there's no reason in the world why that decision should be altered. I'm 100 percent sure of it. Even if an angel of the Lord came down from heaven right now and told me I was really looking at someone else, I would tell the angel he was mistaken. I might even think he was outright lying to me and therefore wonder if he was a demon. But those are the only two options: either the angel would be making a mistake or lying to me. The only thing outside the realm of possibility would be for me to believe I was wrong about who was bringing me a cup of coffee.

Well, that's exactly the kind of certitude Satan and the rebel angels had when they chose to reject God's will. Because they were pure spirits, they didn't need to weigh all the variables. They didn't need to do any research on what life would be like without God. They didn't need any more data about hell. They didn't need to explore all their other options. They saw everything at once; they saw all the consequences of their choice in a flash of angelic vision. And they simply didn't care.

In fact, they had even more certitude than I do about my wife bringing me a cup of coffee, because there's always a chance I might be delusional or sick in some way. Angels, with their amazingly superior intellects, can never be delusional or sick. This is what made their fall so terrible. Because of their spiritual perfection and their powers of insight, they were able to know God in a much more direct way than we do; they were able see much more clearly his greatness than we can. Though angels are not omniscient,[12] their knowledge about God, completely unhampered by the limits of physical senses, is incomparably deeper and richer than ours. And yet, despite this knowledge, despite all the consequences they clearly foresaw, they still rejected him.

And what were the consequences?

We'll be going into greater detail about this later, but for now, let's just say that in rejecting God, the devil rejected truth, because God is truth. In so doing, he became a "liar and the father of lies."[13] In rejecting God, the devil and the demons rejected goodness, because God is goodness. Instead, they embraced all that was evil and hurtful and painful in creation. In rejecting God, the devil and his demons rejected light and life, because God is light and life. Thus they sank into the abyss of darkness and eternal death of the spirit that we call hell.[14]

Do they regret this decision? Do they care that they live in hell? The short answer is no, not in the slightest. In fact, they would rather be in hell than anywhere else in creation. Not that they are happy or joyful in any way, but in a certain sense they do like being where they are, at least in terms of preferring it to the alternative: being with God in heaven. The fact that life in hell entails great suffering only adds to their resentment of God. It only adds to their prideful indignation at being victimized. It only adds fuel to their bitterness and hatred. It only makes them want to offend God more.

How could all this be? How could the devil and the demons reject good and embrace evil? How could they prefer hell to heaven? We actually talked about this at length in the last chapter. Human beings do it all the time. Human beings have made this same decision to reject good and embrace evil throughout their long history. Think again of the Nazis and Stalin and the medical experiments on children and all those killers and rapists and terrorists and their acts of cruelty. Think of all the times in your own life you have made choices that were evil. And recall the times when you preferred to stew in resentment and self-pity rather than reverse your behavior in humility. We've all been there before, to one degree or another. It's just a fact we have to face. As long as you have free will, it's possible to will evil. It's possible to prefer suffering to joy.

The difference between human beings and fallen angels is that we have the power to acknowledge that we made a mistake, that we were ignorant of the facts, that we didn't truly understand what we were doing, that we were flat-out wrong. The demons can't do that because they *did* know what they were doing. They *were* sure of their actions. They *don't* think they were wrong.

This is so important for us to grasp. The devil doesn't think he was wrong for rebelling against God. He thinks he was correct in following his own will. Many theologians speculate that God gave the angels a glimpse of his divine plan for humanity at the very beginning of creation and the devil vehemently opposed it. If that's true (and we'll talk more about that later), then there is some kind of twisted, evil logic to the devil's malevolent choice. In fact, if you could sit the devil down across from you right now and actually get him to be honest, he would insist that *he* was the victim, that *he* was the one who was treated unjustly by God. He would say with 100 percent certitude that God had no right to subject him and the other angels to some kind of bogus free-will test, that God had no right to ask him and the other angels to take part in the building up of his sham kingdom. A kingdom where human beings—infinitely inferior to angels in terms of their natural abilities—would eventually get to reign with God as the book of Revelation prophesies,[15] a kingdom where God himself would stoop so unbelievably low as to *become human* in the person of Jesus Christ. In other words, if you could sit Satan down in front of you right now, he would tell you that he objected to the so-called divine plan from the very beginning. That it's not wrong for him to have rejected God and everything associated with God since God was being so blatantly unfair.

This is how Satan felt at the time of his fall from grace, and that's how he feels now. He's never changed his mind, and he never will. He can't, because he *doesn't have a mind to change*. He is pure spirit, and that spirit has already made its once-and-for-all, forever decision. This is the key to understanding why the devil and his demons aren't going to suddenly come over to our side. It's the key to understanding why all the decisions made by pure spirits are irrevocable. It's also the key to understanding the enigma of hell and its everlasting nature.

Hell isn't just some place God arbitrarily created to imprison creatures that disobeyed him and needed punishment. Hell exists because there are creatures there who made a permanent decision to get as far away from God as possible, no matter the consequences. Hell exists not because God wanted it, but because the rebellious angels did. In a very real sense *they invented hell*, and now that they have, they have no desire to leave.

"But what about us?" you ask. Even if we accept the fact that the devil and his demons are permanently separated from God, how does that have any impact on human beings and our ever-lasting destinies? Demons may be pure spirits, without the ability to change their minds, but surely we can. Why, then, must some of us be doomed to suffer in hell forever?

To answer that question, we must take the next step in our journey, and it is a frightening step indeed. We must examine what transpires during that most fateful and mysterious of all human events: the moment when our souls separate from our bodies, the moment of our earthly deaths. Specifically, we must focus on what happens to our free will at that precise point where time and eternity finally meet.

three

Halfway to Hell

The Moment of Death

Though death is an uncomfortable subject to talk about, I'm afraid there's no way to avoid it on a trip to hell. It's the gateway, after all, to eternal life. It's the door through which we all must pass at some point, no matter how rich or powerful or famous or intelligent we might be. As the saying goes, no one gets out of this life alive.

But death means many things to many people. For some it is a source of incredible anxiety and paralyzing fear. For others it represents liberation from the "whips and scorns of time," a respite from old age and infirmity and pain. For others it means a chance to finally see beloved friends or family who have passed on. For others it is just another step in the great adventure of life, a transition to something new and exciting and unknown. For some it is not a transition at all but rather the total cessation of consciousness and life—nothingness, annihilation, a full stop.

However you look at death, though, one thing is certain: it is mysterious.

According to Christian theology, death has always been defined in a very simple and straightforward way. It is the *separation of the soul from the body*.[1] As we've already briefly discussed, there are three basic kinds of creation. First, there is the material world: the planets, the stars, and all the inanimate objects in the universe. Second, there is the spiritual world: angels, both good and fallen. And finally there is a kind of hybrid creature known as a human being, who is both spirit *and* matter.

That spiritual part of humans is called the soul. It can be described as that invisible entity or principle by which we think and choose and by which our bodies have life. This idea that humans have souls is not something strictly Christian in origin. People of many different religions and no religion at all have inferred the existence of the soul simply from observing life, from observing the mysteries of birth and consciousness and death, the operation of the imagination and memory, the creation of art and music, the capacity we have to reason and to make moral decisions, the inexplicability of humor and laughter. All of this suggests the existence of some force besides the visible human organism, internal to it but in some way independent from it.[2]

Christianity teaches that once deprived of this soul, the human person dies. The departure of the soul from the body actually constitutes the departure of life itself.

Thus the soul is considered the animating principle of the body.

That doesn't mean, however, that death is caused by the soul leaving the body. As everyone knows, it is the failure of the bodily mechanism through deterioration or disease or trauma, followed by death, which initiates the separation of body and soul. Essentially the body stops functioning and the soul leaves as a result. In theory, death could occur the other way around. If the soul of a healthy human being were to suddenly leave its healthy body, that person would go limp and die despite having a perfectly working physiology. But in practice, souls do not leave healthy bodies. What happens is the body breaks down first and is no longer able to *sustain* the soul. Human beings were created by God to be perfect combinations of matter and spirit. So when the matter fails, the spirit must flee.

The critical point to note is that since the substance of the soul is spiritual and not material, it does not die when it leaves the body. Rather it stays alive. Spirits never die. Just like the angels, once a human soul is created by God, it is immortal.[3]

The question is this: What exactly happens to the soul at the moment of separation from the body?

And here we must bring together two strands of thought that we have discussed over the last two chapters. First, we must examine again the idea that human beings have the capacity to make evil choices and remain obstinate in that evil. Second, we must review the idea that when pure spirits make decisions, those decisions are irrevocable and eternal because of the very nature of spiritual choices. Taken together, these two ideas help to explain why some human beings go to hell and stay there forever.

Let's take these concepts one at a time. We talked in the first chapter about the capability we all have for evil. We may never commit murder or perform acts of tremendous cruelty, but we all have within us the seeds for such cruelty. We all have the capability for evil. Sometimes this evil potential is more apparent than at other times. But it usually manifests itself in selfishness, in egotism, in prideful indignation, and in the attempts we make to raise ourselves higher than others at their expense. In actuality, this behavior is contrary to the virtue of love, because love, by definition, is selfless giving and sacrifice for others. Thus, anytime we purposely and unjustly drag others down (in thoughts, words, or deeds), we are committing a sin against love.

Now most times we repent of this sin. Most times we feel guilty, recognize that we have done something wrong, and resolve to do better. If we fall several times, we are apt to get discouraged and sometimes even sink into despair. But usually we rebound from these moral setbacks. In fact, Christianity teaches that, throughout our lives, God continually provides us with help to nudge us away from evil. This help is called grace, and it comes in many forms: direct inspiration from God, assistance from his angels, insights gained from the Bible and other spiritual writings, habits of thinking and trusting gained from suffering, encouragement from conversation with friends, spiritual strength through certain sacraments of the church, even the direct, radical intervention of the Holy Spirit. As long as we are living and breathing, God always gives us the opportunity to come back to his side with grace.[4] We're really involved in a great cosmic game of spiritual tug-of-war. Evil pulls at us in one direction, and God pulls us in the other, even when we've fallen flat on our faces.

And usually it works. We usually come to our senses and realize we're in the wrong, and then either apologize for our bad behavior or at least admit to ourselves that we need to improve.

Essentially, we turn back to God, according to the lights we have been given, and manage to overcome evil—at least for a time. This is what constitutes the Christian meaning of the word *repentance*. And it is a strong indication that though we may be sinners, we are not hardened sinners. We are not confirmed or fixed in our sins.

However, there are times when it's not so easy to repent and reverse direction. There are times when we instead prefer to stay entrenched in our sinfulness. There are times when, as the Bible says, we prefer the darkness to the light.[5]

We talked about this earlier, but it's important to get ourselves into that same evil mind-set again. Think for a moment about some of the times when you have been guilty of prideful obstinacy. Have you ever had a nasty altercation or disagreement with someone and refused to make up? Maybe this person was a coworker or a family member or a neighbor. Maybe this person actually had the nerve to think *you* were at fault? Do you remember thinking to yourself, *I will never apologize to this person! Never!*

I'm not speaking now of the anger you felt when the conflict was first initiated. I'm talking about afterward, when all the heated emotions had subsided, when the only thing preventing reconciliation was the fact you didn't think you did anything wrong and were perfectly content to remain in a state of war.

Can you remember a time in your life when you felt this way and actually *were* the one at fault, when *you* were the one who was wrong and it was only your stubbornness and pride that prevented you from making up? Can you remember a time when you knew you were wrong but didn't care? A time when you actually preferred to be resentful and full of animosity, despite the fact that you were to blame?

As we said in chapter 1, the truth is that sometimes it feels good to be upset. Sometimes humans would rather be upset than anything else in the world. They'd rather stew in a state of miserable contempt than go through the trouble of admitting they were wrong and restoring peace. Sometimes it's just more pleasurable to be mean-spirited and prideful than it is to be merciful and loving, despite whatever grace we receive from God. Indeed, it is this very obstinacy that shuts the door to grace. God might be trying his best through his inspiration, his Word, his church, and his human and angelic messengers to get you to make the right choice. But ultimately it's possible to say no to grace, to make a hellish choice. We do it more times than we'd like to admit. And this is exactly the kind of steadfastness in sin and hardness of heart that we need to keep in mind now as we move to the second strand of thought necessary to understand hell.

We talked in chapter 2 about the difference between decisions made by angels and those made by human beings. Angels, being pure spirits, do not have brains and nervous systems through which their thoughts need to be filtered. They see ideas intuitively, immediately, and completely, without having to go through any process of deliberation and without having to deal with any environmental or genetic biases. Therefore, their faculty of will can operate freely and instantaneously. In a flash, they simply see ideas and choose.

The upshot is that when an angel decides to reject God, that decision is irrevocable, because there's nothing for the angel to ever reconsider. He intuits all possible reasons and consequences at the very start. Since he is a pure spirit, the angel doesn't ever experience any growth or maturity of character that might give him a greater ability to see his error. And since he never receives any new information, there's never any reason for him to modify his decisions. An angel can't change his mind for the simple reason that he has no mind to change.

All of this is ground we've already covered, but now we come to a very tricky question. What happens to us at the moment of death, when our souls disconnect from our bodies? What happens when those souls transition into being pure spirits, without brains and nervous systems? What happens when the choosing mechanism of our will is stripped naked and is no longer tied to any material organism, no longer slowed down by physiological processes or biased by genetic and environmental factors?

This is a very mysterious subject, and we need to consider it carefully. Christianity has always taught that, at the moment of death, the human soul undergoes judgment on all the actions it has ever taken in its earthly existence.[6] We'll talk specifically about the nature of this judgment in the next chapter, but for now just understand the whole notion of judgment presupposes that when we pass the moment of death, we no longer have the ability to influence our fate, to make a choice for or against God, to say yes or no to grace, to do good or evil, to have faith or not to have faith in Christ. All our power to alter our actions and decisions has come to an end. The time of testing is over. Essentially, our *bodily choosing clock* has stopped.

Why? The reason is that, at the very instant of its separation from the body, the human soul begins to live in the same manner as a pure spirit. Its decisions become unchangeable. And the unchangeable, irrevocable decision the soul makes when it first leaves its body is *whatever decision it made when it was last joined with its body.*

Pay close attention here! At the moment of death, we become similar to angels.[7] With the body gone, all that is left are the intellect and the will that constitute the soul. When that soul is separated from the physical mechanism to which it's been united for so long, it is no longer able to reverse course. Remember, it is our weak, inefficient bodies that cause us to waffle in our decision-making. They're what make us go back and forth in our choices a million times. But that very weakness—the thing that makes us inferior to the angels in terms of our inability to know things instantaneously—is also what gives us so much *time* to make our choice about God when we are on earth.

But our time runs out at death. The state of our souls at the moment of separation determines our *final* choice about God. Once death comes, all processes of deliberation end abruptly. As humans, we make our decisions in slow motion, but the decision we freely arrive at by the time we die is the one that counts: it's the one that is frozen. Our earthly obstinacy in either good or evil carries over, as if by momentum. At the moment of death, the soul's will becomes immobile and fixes itself forever in its final choice—either for or against God. Like a tree that falls in the forest, wherever it hits the ground is where it stays.

To make this point even clearer, let's take a close-up look at the soul of someone who actually goes to hell.

The unfortunate human being in question hasn't simply made a mistake or given in to the temptations of the flesh. He has knowingly made a series of free choices in his life to reject the grace of God and the gift of faith. He has also knowingly made a series of free choices in his life to do seriously evil things and to persist in that evil. Deep inside this person's soul, and completely independent of all environmental and genetic considerations, his will has continually rejected God's will. When God gave this person the inspiration to repent, he said no. When opportunities to indulge in grave evil presented themselves, this person gave his free consent. In other words, long before this person's soul separated from his body, a state of evil obstinacy had begun to take hold of it and actually *changed* it.

C. S. Lewis described this process of transformation well:

> Every time you make a choice you are turning the central part of you, the part of you that chooses, into something a little different than it was before. And taking your life as a whole, with all your innumerable choices, all your life long you are slowly turning this central thing either into a heavenly creature or into a hellish creature: either into a creature that is in harmony with God, and with other creatures, and with itself, or else into one that is in a state of war and hatred with God, and with its fellow creatures, and with itself. To be the one kind of creature is heaven: that is, it is joy and peace and knowledge and power. To be the other means madness, horror, idiocy, rage, impotence, and eternal loneliness. Each of us at each moment is progressing to the one state or the other.[8]

A person who continually refuses God's grace and chooses instead to fester in evil is one who will increasingly and inevitably take on the hellish qualities of the devil and his demons. He will continually choose to lie, to accuse, to detract, to be selfish, to pridefully take offense, to engage in cynicism, hopelessness, and a general rebellion against joy and life and God's divine plan. And as his capacity for evil becomes greater with every unrepented sin, so his hidden soul becomes more soiled. If confronted with the truth about himself, this person will invariably express denial and outrage and flatly refuse to accept responsibility or recognize the need to change. On the outside, this person may be able to hide the truth and even successfully fool others into believing that he is good. He may camouflage his coal-black soul with a pretty, pleasant, and affable exterior. He may even mask his true selfishness with attention-getting acts of generosity. But God knows better. God sees inside the person and knows how hypocritical and twisted and dark his soul has actually become.

Now what happens to a person like this at the moment of death? What happens to this person's obstinately evil soul? Some people believe that just before the soul separates from the body— even perhaps milliseconds before death and even if the person is unconscious—God gives one last chance, one final infusion of grace, in the hope that it will turn around in faith and repentance. But that's just speculation. No one knows for sure what happens between God and a human being who has just shuffled off this mortal coil. The only thing Christianity teaches with absolute certitude is that if a person is lost, it is *not* through any lack of mercy on God's part. Somehow, some way, God gives every person the *chance* to repent, just as he offers every person the *gift* of faith.[9] Whether that chance or that gift is accepted is totally up to the individual.

Once the moment of death arrives, however, three things automatically happen. The first is that all grace from God stops. Grace is the help human beings receive from God on their voyage through earthly life. But once that voyage comes to an end, there is no more help from God. The time for mercy is over; the time for justice has begun. At death, human beings are no longer given any more inspirations from God, any nudges from his angels, any pull on their souls to help them get back up. They are finally left alone by God, left alone with the result of their own free choice, left alone with their own decrepit human nature divorced from grace. They have nothing else.

Second, that choice—whatever it is—becomes fixed. A human soul that has remained intransigent in rejecting God's grace during its life on earth now becomes a soul whose decision is as immutable as that of the devil and his demons. Christians call this choice final impenitence and identify it with the infamous sin against the Holy Spirit that Christ spoke of in the Gospels.[10] It is the one and only sin that cannot be forgiven, because the soul *does not want to be forgiven*. Rather, the soul is locked into the same hatred of God's will that it had on earth, only now with no possibility of turning around. Indeed, it has no *desire* to turn around. As a pure spirit, free of its fickle body, it wants to go on forever being obstinate and prideful and deceitful and accusatory and resentful and outraged and fallen.

And that is the third thing that happens to an impenitent soul upon separation from its body. It falls. How and where, exactly, does it fall? That is the next step in our journey.

Falling Like Lightning

What Judgment Really Means

I warn you, the next few chapters are liable to be challenging. If you dislike theology, you might be tempted to skip through them. That's okay. But if you really want to understand how and why people are damned to hell, then it's worth going slowly, even though it might seem a bit tedious at times. You must have a solid foundation in the theology of judgment for any of this to be comprehensible. So let's avoid the temptation to take any shortcuts and go over the subject carefully.

God wills that all people be saved.[1] And yet we know many people are not. How can that be? If God is all-powerful and his will is sovereign, how in the world can human beings or angels override God's will? How can they choose hell? The answer is one of the great mysteries of Christianity and has to do with the subject of providence.

Providence basically means that God created everything, knows everything, and is in charge of everything. Simply put, it means that whatever God wants, God gets.[2] And yet in his desire to share his happiness in the greatest possible way, God gave human beings and angels the gift of free will. Only by having free will can we really partake in God's joy. If we didn't have free will, we would just be glorified robots.

And this is where the mystery comes in. God wants us to be good, and yet he allows us to make evil choices, even to sin grievously against him. He allows Satan and the demons and Judas and Hitler to indulge their evil desires. He allows them (and all of us) to go against his will. Standing outside of time and space, God sees our freely made evil choices from all eternity and arranges them in such a way that a greater good is brought out of them. Thus, even though Pontius Pilate and the Pharisees freely conspired to commit the greatest evil in all history—the murder of Christ—God still found a way to pull the greatest good from it, namely, the resurrection of Christ and the opening of the gates of heaven. Somehow, some way, God always makes sure his sovereign will prevails without taking away one iota from the freedom of our individual wills. How he does this—how he arranges our free choices so they ultimately conform and even contribute to the fulfillment of his divine plan—is a mystery beyond our comprehension. But it is part of the Christian faith.

The bottom line is that God never forces someone into hell. He is almighty, but he allows us to choose against him, even to choose hell. As G. K. Chesterton said, "Hell is God's great compliment to the reality of human freedom and the dignity of human choice."[3]

However, as we've said previously, once our earthly lives come to an end, so, too, do all our choices. The time for judgment is at hand. And that is the subject we are going to tackle in this chapter.

The Bible clearly implies the souls of human beings are judged the very moment they are separated from their bodies. In the famous parable of the rich man and Lazarus, Christ makes it clear that both men received their respective punishment and reward immediately after death.[4] Likewise, to the "good thief" hanging on the cross next to him, Christ promised that he would soon be among the blessed: "Truly I tell you, today you will be with me in paradise."[5]

Though justice is often delayed and denied in this world, that will not be the case in the next. After you die, justice will be swift and sure. If you have ever witnessed a person's death, you know what a solemn event it is, not only because the person is leaving this world forever but also because of the momentous fact that at that very instant—even though it is invisible to your eyes—the soul of the deceased is standing before the judgment seat of God.

Christianity has always taught that there are actually two separate, distinct forms of judgment. The first is what we started to discuss in the last chapter and is known as the particular judgment because it has to do with what happens to a particular soul at the moment of death.[6] But there is also something called the Last Judgment, which is the subject of Michelangelo's famous fresco in the Sistine Chapel. This judgment will take place at the end of time, after what is known as the resurrection of the dead, when all souls are finally reunited with their bodies.[7] We'll be talking a lot about the Last Judgment and what happens to human beings as a result of it throughout the remainder of this book. For now, though, we must continue to examine the state of a soul that has been damned when it separates from its earthly body. Its final decision to reject God has been fixed as immutably as the decision of Satan and the other fallen angels.

But what happens next?

First of all, it is imperative to understand that once a soul is freed from its body, it is still very much *alive*. It doesn't die. There is not a single second when it is "nonexistent" or "annihilated" or "nothing." Christianity teaches that the human soul has a beginning but no end. It was created by God to be immortal. As the animating principle of the body, it is the very force that gives it life and allows it to breathe and move and think. So when it leaves the body, it has no problem existing on its own. That's what a soul does. It *lives*.[8]

Being alive, it is also *aware*. It is *conscious*. In some fashion, it is able to "see." Not with the eyes, of course, but through some spiritual means of intuition that we have no way of understanding.

Remember, the angels can see and they don't have eyes. God the Father can see and he doesn't have eyes. And you yourself can see when you're dreaming and your eyes are shut. That's because when you're sleeping you can still look at things with your mind and with your imagination.

A similar principle is involved here. Though the soul does not, properly speaking, have a mind or imagination, it nevertheless enjoys the faculty of vision. Sight is a power that comes from God, and he doesn't take that power away from us when we die. It so happens that when you're alive and possess a body, the seeing mechanism is carried out through the physical senses—through the optic nerve and retina and pupil and cornea and iris, all of which relay images to the brain. But that filtering system actually slows down the process of vision. When the soul is separated from the body, there won't be any physiological limitations, and the ability of the soul to see will be much more direct, immediate, and powerful.

Many people are afraid that when they die they're going to be immersed in darkness. After all, when you close your eyes, it's dark. And when we see a person who is dead, his or her eyes are closed. So it's easy to make that connection between darkness and death. But not only is the connection false, it is the very opposite of the truth. After death, there is not one moment of darkness. According to the Bible and every tradition within Christianity, God is light.[9] And his kingdom is a kingdom of light. When human beings die, they are not plunged into some kind of black hole. Death doesn't resemble unconsciousness in any way. It's nothing like being in a dark room. It's nothing like nighttime. The instant a person dies, he or she has an encounter with the living God and, as a result, sees the light that proceeds from God. It is a light of profound intellectual illumination. And it is a light that either brings comfort, peace, and consolation or, in the case of a damned soul, burning pain.

It is this light that constitutes the essence of what Christians call judgment, because it is a light that illuminates the whole truth about reality, including the truth about the soul itself.

At the very instant of death, everything that was previously hidden from the soul in earthly life suddenly becomes clear. For the first time, the soul is able to see the invisible truth about itself. It sees itself as it really is, as God sees it. It sees the good, the bad, and the ugly. It sees exactly how much of its life on earth was given over to love and exactly how much was given over to selfishness and sin. It sees all that it has ever thought, desired, spoken, done, and not done. It sees it all in a flash of penetrating light.

This is an important point to grasp. When the newly separated soul is exposed to the light of God and sees itself for what it actually is, it retains its identity. In other words, when you die, you will still be *you*. You will know who you are and what has happened to you. You won't suddenly get amnesia in the afterlife. In fact, your memory and conscience will extend even further—to your whole moral and spiritual past and down to the minutest detail. You will be able to see who you are at the very core of your being. The particular judgment is this moment of radical self-revelation.

This is one of the biggest differences between Christianity and Eastern religions such as Buddhism and Hinduism. According to those faiths, human beings don't have any kind of permanent identity. When you die, whoever you were in life ceases to exist. Your spirit may continue on in some other way or reincarnate in some other form, but it won't truly be *you*. Like a drop of water immersed in the ocean, the human soul loses its individuality after it passes from this life.

Christianity, on the other hand, teaches the exact opposite.[10] In the next life, not only will you continue to be yourself, but you'll actually become *more* of who you really are. Your true personality—your best you—is what lives on in heaven. Likewise, if you reject God, your worst you—essentially what remains of your identity after your choice to embrace evil and after your phony, pretty exterior has been burned off—is what lives on forever in hell.

As we discussed in the previous chapter, for a soul that is damned, judgment actually consists of several distinct, simultaneous phases. First, the soul's final decision about God becomes fixed and unchangeable. Second, all grace from God stops. Third, the soul is exposed to and infused with a light from God that enables it to clearly see the decision it has made to reject God. This light also reveals to the soul all the other evil choices it made in life. Thus the soul fully recognizes its depravity. Fourth, by virtue of this free choice, the soul falls into hell.

This is a very different picture of judgment than the cartoonish idea so many people have about it. Even Christians are guilty of misunderstanding the concept of God's judgment. Many of them believe that when someone dies, God is waiting at the pearly gates with the spiritual equivalent of a big stick in his hands, ready to pounce on that person for all his sins. And if those sins are serious enough, he is eager to pronounce a sentence and open some kind of trapdoor through which the person plummets to eternal hellfire.

But this is not the case. As the apostle Paul said of those being judged, "The requirements of the law are written on their hearts, their consciences also bearing witness, and their thoughts sometimes accusing them and at other times even defending them. This will take place on the day when God judges people's secrets through Jesus Christ, as my gospel declares."[11]

In other words, judgment should never be conceived of as a form of vengeance inflicted by God from the outside. Rather, it is something that results from the very nature of sin and our own awareness of our free-will decision to embrace it. Thus, when it comes to the particular judgment, God doesn't have to pronounce a sentence at all. Yes, a judgment is made and a sentence issued. But there is never any conflict between the opinion of the court and the opinion of the defendant.

In fact, the process is not like anything that goes on in earthly courtrooms, where a human tribunal or judge examines a case, announces a verdict, pronounces a sentence, and then executes the sentence. Far from it. In God's court, there is no anticipation or worry or dread while the defendant awaits the decision of the Judge. The sentencing of a soul to hell does not come from any kind of booming voice that can be heard by the ear. Judgment is purely a matter of *intellectual illumination*, whereby a soul sees all the actions of its past life, sees God's judgment of those actions, sees clearly that it has rejected God, and as a natural outcome of that rejection, *desires* separation from God. In other words, the decision of the soul is in complete conformity, harmony, and agreement with the judgment of God. A soul that has rejected God *wants* to remove itself from God's presence. The soul thus falls into hell of its own volition.

Let's focus more on this word *falling* for a moment. Why do the Scriptures always speak of the devil and the demons as falling? Why, for instance, did the prophet Isaiah say: "How you have fallen from heaven, O Lucifer, son of the dawn."[12] And why in the gospel of Luke does Christ say: "I saw Satan falling like lightning from heaven."[13]

Obviously since a soul is a pure spirit and doesn't have a body, it is impossible for it to fall in the way a human being does. Clearly, we are dealing with a metaphor. But a good metaphor, while not literally accurate, conveys a tremendous amount of truth, even the essence of truth. For example, the great thirteenth-century theologian Thomas Aquinas said that virtue was analogous to lightness and sin to heaviness. Things that are light will naturally rise, while things that are heavy will fall. Thus, love of God and neighbor, like a flame, rises upward to heaven, while hatred of God and neighbor, like a leaden weight, descends to hell.

But there's more to this metaphor than just a directional component. A fall of a soul into hell also means a pulling back from God, a falling away. It represents the desire of a soul to withdraw an infinite distance from what it hates. The metaphor also conveys the idea of speed. The soul does not just retreat from God, it does so like lightning.

How can we understand this better?

When a person rebels against God, even in this life, there is a natural, built-in reaction. It's similar to when you put your hand in a fire. When you do that, you get burned immediately. There's nothing that happens in between. There's no secondary action required for you to feel that burning sensation. Your brain doesn't have to make any decisions. It's not a slow process. It just occurs as a consequence of your action. And if you keep your hand in the fire long enough, even more painful things will happen. Your flesh will burn and turn different colors and even begin to fall off.

It's the same with sinning. Anytime you rebel against God, there is an automatic reaction, a reaction that can be described as disintegration or disorder or darkening of the spirit.[14] The reaction may not be immediately visible, but at some point in time, it results in pain and isolation and brokenness and unhappiness. God doesn't have to *do* anything to make you feel those things. He doesn't have to send any thunderbolts from heaven. It's just part of the built-in mechanism that comes along with having free will. When you abuse your free will to rebel against God, there are natural consequences that simply *must* follow. It's a law of the universe every bit as certain as gravity.

Why? Because if you turn away from God, you're essentially turning away from everything that God is. We touched on this earlier. It means that since God is light, turning away from him is going to plunge you into darkness. Since God is order, turning away from him is going to cause you to experience chaos. Since God is wisdom, turning away from him is going to result in confusion. Since God is peace, turning away from him is going to cause strife. Since God is beauty, turning away from him is going to mean that things in your life get messy and ugly. This is just common sense. The punishment we receive as a result of sinning doesn't have anything to do with God getting back at us. It has to do with the disintegration and darkness and disorder that automatically results from rebelling against God.

Now, if you've made a lifelong habit of rebelling against God and you're still not sorry—even at the point of death—that's going to have an automatic consequence too. If you've rejected the grace God has given you freely, if you've refused to love God and your neighbors the way we're all called to do, if you've gotten to the end of your life and your attitude is still "I don't care what God wants, it's what *I* want that counts," then it's obvious what's going to happen. Your separated soul—now fixed and immutable in its decision against God—is going to be bathed in the harsh light of truth, with all its sins exposed, and by virtue of its own free choice, it's going to immediately turn away from God the same way it did on earth. It's going to *want* to flee. It's going to *want* to run. It's going to *want* to pull back and fall away. Only this time, the falling away will be forever.

Here's a good way to understand how the judgment of the

damned works. Try thinking about a time when you weren't doing well spiritually, when you were indulging in a particular sin and knew you were wrong but weren't ready to stop. When you were in that kind of unspiritual and rebellious state, did you feel very much like praying? Did you feel like reading the Bible? Did you feel like going to church? Did you feel like thinking about God? What was your general attitude toward things and activities that had to do with spirituality? You probably wanted nothing to do with them, correct?

I can tell you from personal experience that when I've been in the grips of some particularly attractive sin and haven't been very willing to repent and reverse course, the *last* thing I wanted to do was think about God. During those times, I didn't want to see anything that remotely reminded me of God. If I were watching television, for instance, and accidentally came across someone holding a Bible and preaching, I couldn't switch channels fast enough. If I passed by a church on the street, I avoided looking at it. If I was glancing through books in my office or on my tablet and saw a spiritual classic, I passed over it quickly. Anything that reminded me of God was painful, because it forced me to confront my own bad behavior, which I didn't want to do. Thankfully, I don't experience that phenomenon as much as I used to, but I remember plenty of times in my life when I did.

But what if these weren't just moral lapses or sinful binges or simple falls? What if, instead of just doing evil occasionally, you came to *love* evil? What if your soul became so twisted that it actually began to hate what is good? What if your aversion to God and all things that reminded you of God became something permanent? What if you got to the end of your life and you were still stuck in that hardened, unrepentant, unfaithful state?

The answer is that the same exact thing that happened when you were alive and sinful is going to happen when you're dead and sinful. You're going to see the light from God and you're going to run in the opposite direction. The light won't be beautiful or warm or inviting. It will be painful. It will be hurtful. It will convict you of all your sins. You're not going to be able to stand looking at it. You're going to want to get away from it as fast as you can. In fact, you're going to dive straight into hell. That's going to be your natural, instantaneous reaction—and God won't have to lift one of his divine fingers to point the way.

That is what is really meant by the terms *falling* and being *judged*.

The questions are: Where exactly does the soul fall? When it lands, what does it feel? What does it suffer? How can it even experience such things if it doesn't have a body?

And this is where the tour of hell really starts, because this is where the pain begins.

Avoiding a Wrong Turn

How to Make Sense of Spiritual Suffering

B efore we discuss the actual pain a soul suffers in hell, we must first pause to answer what some might consider a tedious, mechanical question: How can a soul feel pain in the first place? After all, a soul is spiritual, while pain is mostly a physical or emotional phenomenon.

It is imperative we undertake this discussion in a step-by-step fashion, even if it seems a bit laborious. The reason is twofold. First, the Christian teaching on hell is not very easy to comprehend, and it builds logically, piece by piece. Second, this is not just a book on hell; it's a *travel guide*. That means if we make one wrong turn, one slight deviation, it might lead us in a completely different direction. That's something we can't allow. We can't take shortcuts on this tour. We can't go the wrong way. Hell is too important a topic. Not enough people believe in it or take it seriously enough. It's incumbent upon all Christians to really try their best to understand how someplace so terrible can exist and how God can allow people to go there. If we don't take the time and trouble to think about hell, do you know what will happen? *More* people will go there.

So to pick up where we left off in the last chapter, the doomed soul we've been talking about has just separated from its body, experienced judgment, and of its own accord turned away from God, in essence leaving God's presence and falling into hell.

Now, because we are talking about a pure spirit, terms like "turning," "leaving," and "falling" cannot be taken literally. The spiritual realm has no spatial or geographic component. Therefore the best we can say is that the reprobate soul has freely chosen to reject God, thereby shutting itself off from God, similar to when we shut our eyes or put our hands in front of our faces to block the light or avoid seeing something that displeases or frightens us. The point is not so much to understand exactly how spiritual entities do this but to accept they do indeed have that power. During judgment, they can turn away from God and go to hell without moving one inch.

Remember, most Christians believe that human beings undergo *two* judgments. The first occurs at the moment we die, and it is specific to the individual human being. A person's soul leaves its body and instantaneously becomes aware of the final decision it has made in earthly life—to accept or reject God. This is called the particular judgment, and as a result, the soul goes either to heaven or hell (again, we are not discussing the possibility of purgatory here, which Catholics believe to be part of heaven, a cleansing process before seeing God face-to-face).

After the particular judgment, the damned soul immediately experiences some of the pains of hell. I say *some* because, at this point, the soul is separated from its body and cannot experience bodily suffering. Later on, at the end of time, there will be another judgment, called the Last Judgment. We'll be devoting a whole chapter to this later, but the only thing we need to know now is that, at the Last Judgment, the soul is not really judged again. No reevaluation or reconsideration of the past ever takes place. The judgment we undergo at the moment of death is permanent and irrevocable. At the Last Judgment, what mainly happens is our souls are *reunited* with our bodies and then publicly confirmed in whatever judgment has already been made. We become whole human beings again and begin to experience heaven or hell in a different, more physical way and in a more physical place.

The questions for us to consider are these: What happens to the soul in hell *before* it is reunited with its body at the Last Judgment? What kind of suffering does it experience when it is in this purely spiritual state? As we just said, a soul can't experience physical pain. When the Bible and the great saints and spiritual writers of the past describe hell in terms of flames of unquenchable fire, which burn without consuming,[1] they are not speaking of an actual earthly fire, at least not in reference to hell before the resurrection. After all, it's impossible to set a pure spirit on fire—not with a match, not with a blowtorch, not even with a bomb. Fire is the visible effect of a chemical reaction called combustion, occurring between oxygen in the air and some kind of fuel. Fire can only ignite when gasses interact with each other, and gasses are made up of molecules. Obviously, all these things belong to the material world—not the spiritual. Thus, when the Bible refers to hellfire, it either refers to a mysterious form of spiritualized fire that we have no way of understanding or to the fire in hell *after* the resurrection, when human beings will once again have a material component to their makeup.

Yet despite this legitimate question about the nature of hellfire, Christianity teaches with absolute certitude there *is* pain in hell even before human beings get their bodies back. Real spiritual pain. Putting aside the subject of fire for a moment (don't worry, we'll come back to it), let's focus on the kinds of spiritual pains we know a little about. In order to make sense of such suffering, we must first remind ourselves of what a soul is. That's really the key to unlocking the mystery of spiritual pain.

A soul is the immortal, immaterial part of a human being. It's what gives a human being life. It's the animating principle of the body. It is also the seat of the intellect and the will. In other words, the soul gives human beings the ability to reason and to choose. Taken together, these abilities account for why the Bible says that human beings are made in the image and likeness of God,[2] in whom there also exists intellect and will.

However, this definition doesn't quite give the whole story. To simply say the soul is an animating force with the ability to reason and choose makes it seem as if the soul is a cold, robotic entity, one that just thinks thoughts and makes choices about them. The truth is more complex and harder to fathom. The intellect of the soul is not just a computer that reasons, and the animating principle is more than just a life force. Both of these together are the *source* of our consciousness, our memory, our imaginations, our emotions, our ability to make use of our senses, and our conscience. These human faculties do not originate in any bodily organ; they are made possible by the soul.

Our souls are joined with our bodies in such a complete, intimate union that they form one human nature. That means God didn't just stick them together, like two different-colored pieces of clay that are bonded to each other but still retain their distinctive qualities. Rather, he joined the body and soul together so perfectly that they became something totally new.[3] The process is more like the joining of hydrogen and oxygen to form water, a liquid that is very different than either of those two gasses. The soul is thus an incomplete creation without the body, and the body is an incomplete creation without the soul. Both need each other to be a whole human being.

Because of this intimate, substantial, and unique union, it is very difficult for us to separate the distinctive roles of the soul and the body and to define exactly what each contributes to human behavior. Whatever affects the soul affects the body and vice versa. Likewise, the faculties of the soul are all carried out *through* the body.

Practically speaking, this means the soul expresses itself primarily by means of the human brain. For example, we said before the soul is what gives life to the human body. And yet, when brain waves stop, life becomes unsustainable and the person dies. Thus, in a human being, the brain and the soul are inextricably bound together.

We also said before that the soul is rational. Human beings do not get their ability to reason from their brains; they get it from their souls. The brain acts as a kind of processor for the soul's rationality. But the human brain, being physical and quasi-mechanical, does not translate that rationality in a pure, undistilled, and perfect way. The brain is a marvelous but imperfect organ. It has many limitations, and those limitations prevent the soul's rational power from acting instantaneously and comprehensively. Moreover, if the brain becomes disordered in some way—because of an injury or a disease or drugs or a genetic mutation such as Down syndrome—its failure to translate the soul's rationality becomes even more pronounced, and the rational part of the soul will not shine through as effectively as it should. That doesn't mean it's not there, just that it's obscured. In heaven someday, we'll be able to see the true rational power of all human beings—including those who are mentally handicapped—but until then, that ability remains partially hidden.[4]

The same is true for the soul's free will. We've discussed how the brain's physiology—its lobes, cortices, neurons, and synapses—slow down the process of decision-making and make it possible for us to reconsider our choices and change our minds a million times. In addition to this, our habits, moods, stress levels, and a whole slew of environmental factors affect the brain so much that the soul's free will is constantly compromised, to such an extent that only God himself is able to see how truly culpable we are for the sinful choices we make.

What all this means is that the body acts as a filtering mechanism for the main operations of the soul, and thus it prevents us from being able to identify those operations clearly. This is even more evident when it comes to our vision, our imagination, and our emotions. These functions are really wired into the body. Indeed, they are almost impossible to understand apart from human physiology. For instance, we mentioned in the previous chapter that a soul separated from its body can still see, not through the physiological process we're familiar with, in which light and images are projected onto the retina and then relayed by the optic nerve via electrical signals to the brain, but rather through a mysterious spiritual power.

How can we be sure of this? In the Old and New Testaments, it is apparent that angels—who are pure spirits—are able to see and recognize human beings and assist them in various ways. The same ability can be observed in the devil and his demons, who are shown throughout the Scriptures tempting and possessing people.[5] These purely spiritual creatures could not possibly conduct such operations blindly. Somehow, they are aware of and interact with not only corporeal human beings but also other shapeless, formless, invisible beings. In some way they are able to see each other. This could only be possible if the source of vision is the spirit and not the body.

Now, human beings are not angels, but the ability of their souls to see works on the same principle. When we are alive on earth, the seeing process is carried out by the eyes in conjunction with the brain. But when we die, that faculty will be carried out by the soul itself, from which the faculty of vision originates.

Think about that incredible woman Helen Keller, who was both blind and deaf for her entire life. She never heard music. She never saw a sunset. Nor did she ever hear an unkind word or see an act of violence. She lived in total silence and darkness till the moment she died. Today, Helen Keller's soul lives on, hopefully in heaven. One day, though, after the resurrection, she will have a new body, one that is free from all disease and disorder. She'll have eyes that work and ears that function. But Helen Keller doesn't have to wait till the resurrection to see or hear things. Quite the opposite is true. As someone once remarked, despite the tragedy of her life, it's amazing to think that the first sound

Helen Keller ever heard was the voice of God. The first sight she ever beheld was the face of God.

Yes, when Helen Keller died, she *gained* the abilities to hear and to see. That's what Christianity teaches.

The faculty of imagination is also something that will carry on after death, though in a much different way. On earth, human imagination always involves the creation or remembrance of mental images that are manipulated and transmitted through the brain and nervous system. Because of this reliance on the body, a disembodied soul will not have the power to imagine things in the same way we do.

But again, the *source* of human imagination is the soul, because it provides us with the creative spark, the ability to form concepts and images in our minds. Creativity is a God-given talent, a reflection of God's own nature as the Creator.[6] Thus, while it is true that Mozart used and perfected his brain's capacity to imagine musical images to write his symphonies, his actual ability to create was a spiritual gift from God, and as such it resided in his soul. His human imagination, intimately joined to the creative faculty of his soul, is what enabled him to produce his masterpieces in the manner he did—through a series of mental actions involving inspiration, perspiration, composition, and revision. But the power itself originated in his soul. And this is true for all artists.

Now, if a person dies and is damned to hell, his soul will retain that something that gave him the ability to imagine things on earth, just as he will retain that something that gave him the abilities to see and to hear.

A similar point can be made about a person's emotions. Emotions, by definition, are physiological phenomena and are experienced and expressed through the brain, the nervous system, the sensory-motor system, and rest of the body. Souls, as purely spiritual entities, can't get emotional in the way we do. They don't have blood pressure that can rise, adrenal glands that can pump, vocal cords that can shout, mouths that can laugh, or eyes that can cry.

But that doesn't mean human emotions and the soul aren't connected. They are! All emotions arise within the *unity* of body and soul. They are made possible, in part, by our free will, which desires certain things and is sometimes thwarted in those desires, with resultant feelings of repugnance or sorrow.

Neither God nor the angels nor the devil nor the demons are cold or computerlike essences. The devil *hates* God. God *loves* human beings. These are true statements. The spiritual actions of hating and loving may not be the same as their bodily equivalents, but neither are they simple evaluations made by frigid, heartless, superrational intellects. The righteous and mighty anger of God as described in the Old Testament—and even the righteous and mighty anger of Christ in the New Testament—indicate something significant. Yes, the biblical authors articulated anger in human language so human beings could better understand it, but their writing was founded on a great truth: feeling is a gift that comes from God, made possible by the soul working in union with the body.

Or, consider it in another way. The souls of people in heaven are genuinely joyful when they see God and are reunited with the souls of their loved ones. The joy they experience is real and much more similar to human emotion than to any kind of cold, rational appreciation of the goodness of God. Likewise, the souls of people in hell are genuinely hateful and resentful toward God, even before they get their bodies back in the resurrection. That is because, in their earthly lives, they hated God and loved evil. The basis for these emotions was a malicious pride in their souls, and that pride lives on after death and makes the spiritual equivalent of anger and resentment possible in hell.

Thus, while the human soul separated from the body cannot experience emotions as such, since it is ultimately the *source* of all feeling, it is therefore capable of experiencing something *akin to* emotion after death.

Do you get what we're saying here? Do you see what we're driving at? A soul in hell, though totally disconnected from its body, can still experience something similar to sensations, even though it won't employ actual sense organs to experience them. A soul in hell will be able to see and hear and even feel in some manner of speaking. And *that's* why it can experience some form of pain and suffering, even before the resurrection.

Perhaps the best way to illustrate this is to go back to the dream analogy. A person who is asleep is basically motionless. He lies flat on his bed, oblivious to what's going on in the world. His limbs are not being used. His eyes are closed. He doesn't utilize any of his senses in a conscious way. His autonomic nervous system is controlling all his various physiological processes— respiration, digestion, circulation, and so on. Yet, though his senses are in the off position, he may still be dreaming and is therefore capable of experiencing the most lifelike illusions. He can be running. He can be talking. He can be sobbing. He can be listening to music. He can see other people and feel their presence. If he is having a nightmare, he can experience emotions such as fear or envy or discouragement or loneliness or sorrow or even rage. In fact, the things he sees and feels can be so realistic that his blood pressure can become elevated to the point where he actually wakes up crying or screaming.

This analogy gives us a tiny glimpse into how a soul in hell can experience pain before the resurrection. Of course, it is by no means a perfect analogy. In fact, when it comes to spiritual suffering, the nightmare comparison isn't nearly as terrifying as the real thing. After all, when a person has a nightmare, he is still using his imagination, which the soul does not possess, strictly speaking. The imagination is an incredible thing, but it can often serve to obscure a dream's meaning and make its contents seem hazy and random and disconnected. The vision of a soul in hell has no such haziness. When it suffers the spiritual equivalent of great mental, visual, auditory, and emotional torments, it does so with the most intense, realistic clarity. And of course, unlike the pain in a bad dream, which eventually comes to an end, the soul's suffering doesn't ever stop, because it's already wide awake and living its true life.

What are these nightmarish things a soul in hell sees, hears, and feels so clearly? That's the next stop on our tour.

A Preview of Pain

Suffering in Hell Before the Resurrection

As we said at the start of this travel guide, there are souls in hell right now. As you're reading these words, they are suffering in terrible anguish. It's time we talked about that suffering.

In the previous chapter we discussed the various faculties of the soul that enable it, even when disconnected from the body, to maintain its identity, to know itself, to perceive its surroundings, and to experience something similar to vision, hearing, memory, imagination, and emotion. All of this taken together gives the soul in hell the ability to suffer.

For the sake of simplicity, I'm not going to continue emphasizing the difference between earthly and hellish pain. From this point forward, when we speak of a soul in hell feeling a certain kind of misery, what we really mean is that it is experiencing the spiritual equivalent of feeling. We know that feeling is something that is made possible by the soul that manifests itself bodily in our sensory appetites and our human emotions. So when we say a soul in hell feels isolated or envious or hateful, please know we are not talking about human sensory emotions, but rather whatever mysterious phenomenon corresponds to those emotions in pure spirits.

With that proviso in mind, what *kind* of pain do these reprobate souls feel?

The greatest spiritual writers of all time and from every tradition in Christianity agree on one essential point regarding hell: the most intense pain and the chief punishment suffered by the souls of the damned is their eternal separation and self-exclusion from God. God made the human soul in his image, and only in union with God can humans possess the kind of happiness they truly desire. If a soul loses the ability to be in union with God, it essentially loses everything.[1]

Now we read about this pain of loss in all the many books, articles, and essays on hell. But it's still not an easy concept to understand. The only way to really imagine it is by using a variety of imperfect analogies that reveal only small parts of the truth.

For instance, when you turn away from a person you dislike and exclude him or her from your life, you're going to lose whatever is good about that person and that relationship. This happens in families all the time, when different family members fight with each other and then go for years without seeing each other, sometimes till the end of their lives. There's usually a reason for the separation, maybe a good reason, but the separation always involves a loss of some kind. That's because everyone in life has something to offer. If, for whatever reason, you stop talking to your sister or your brother or your cousin, there is going to be a downside. Perhaps you'll be depriving yourself of that person's sense of humor. Perhaps you'll be depriving yourself of having a good relationship with that person's children. Perhaps you'll be losing the ability to see other family members you *do* like during the holidays. The point is this: whatever good is connected to the person is what you're going to lose when that relationship ends. That's just common sense.

The same can be said for a place you dislike. I lived in New York City for many years, and there was a lot about it that I loved, but there was also a lot about it that I hated. Eventually the things I hated became so numerous and so oppressive that I left—a decision I'm very comfortable with today. But that doesn't change the fact that I *did* lose something. I lost all that was good and wonderful and fun about that crazy city. I lost the tremendous variety of restaurants, shows, and museums. I lost all that energy and excitement.

For me the trade-off was worth it. But there *was* a trade-off. It always comes down to a trade-off of some kind. Whenever you say no to something, you also have to say no to a whole host of other related things—some of them good.

But let's look now at the soul of a person in hell who has turned away from God. It goes without saying that this person thought he had good reasons for rejecting God. Perhaps in life he hated God's commandments and laws, or hated the necessity God imposed on him to have faith, or hated God's insistence that he love his neighbors, or hated God's plan for his life, or hated the various crosses and sufferings that God gave him, or hated the very idea of obeying some unseen deity. Whatever the case, he said no to God and he persisted in his no to the very end, right up until the moment when his decision became irrevocable. As we've seen, it's possible for a soul to make such a choice. Yet even if that choice is freely made, there's still something the soul knows it's giving up.

And here we come to the nature of this momentous sacrifice. Exactly what does a soul give up when it gives up God?

For centuries, theologians have tried to describe what the experience of seeing and loving God in heaven will be like. They even have a name for it: *the beatific vision*. In heaven right now the angels and the souls of the blessed are able to see God by direct intuition, clearly and distinctly in a face-to-face manner, with no other created things in between. Here on earth we have no such immediate perception of God. We see him indirectly through the created world, which acts as a kind of mirror for God.[2] We see other creatures around us that bear a likeness to different qualities of God, and then, through reasoning about these creatures and with the help of grace, we are able to come to an understanding of God, albeit a very imperfect understanding.

But in heaven it won't be that way. In heaven we will have immediate, supernatural, face-to-face knowledge of God. And this stupendous beatific vision will give us perfect happiness, because it will be a direct experience of love, truth, goodness, beauty, peace, and home—all at once. By granting us the ability to behold him in this extremely intimate fashion, God doesn't merely satisfy our desire for happiness; he does so in a super-abundant way.[3]

But let's try to unpack this notion of the beatific vision in terms we can understand, especially in terms of what a soul in hell loses by giving it up.

Unlike a person who might possess good qualities or a place that might have good things about it, God is good itself. He is the *source* of all good things.[4] Christianity teaches that the good things we see and experience on earth are merely reflections of different aspects of God, sort of like photographs of God from different angles. The same can be said about everything in life that is beautiful and true. God *is* beauty. He *is* truth.[5] He is the source of those things. Anything beautiful or true that we see on earth or in other human beings is really a reflection of the beauty and truth that is part of God's very identity.

Thus, when you see something that is beautiful—perhaps a baby or a sunrise or a starry night—the reason you know it's beautiful in the first place is because your God-given soul recognizes the beauty of God that exists in those creations. There is one single source of beauty, from which all the things around us derive their beauty. And that single source is God.

The theological explanation is that God is so great, none of his creations can fully reflect him. Instead, they each reflect only a small part of him. Some created objects reflect beauty, others goodness, others truth, all to varying degrees and in different combinations. So if you turn away from a person in your family who has harmed you, there is a possibility there might be some good or true or beautiful thing about that person you have to give up. Likewise, in the case of leaving a place like New York, I had to knowingly sacrifice some of its good and true and beautiful elements. But when a person turns away from God himself, that person is not just turning away from a mere reflection; he is turning away from the very source of all goodness and all truth and all beauty.

That is a sacrifice almost impossible to fathom. People who

reject God reject all that is good in existence, and so they are left with nothing but evil. They reject all that is true in existence, and so they are left with nothing but lies. They reject all that is beautiful in existence, and so they are left with nothing but ugliness.

Can you imagine what a life like that would be like?

And of course, God is also love.[6] Anytime you experience sacrificial giving or intimacy or connection between human beings on earth—apart from sinfulness—you can be sure it is a reflection of God. Thus, if a soul turns away from God permanently, he turns away from the source of all love because he turns away from love itself. What does that leave him with? Nothing but hatred.

Souls in hell are filled with contempt not only for God but for the demons, for the angels, for the blessed in heaven, and for the other souls in hell. There is no friendship or camaraderie among the damned souls in hell, because there is no trace of love left in any of them. Love is what makes friendship and camaraderie possible, even between the great sinners on earth. But in hell no such bond exists. There is only inexpressible resentment, rage, bile, and bitterness, all of which manifests in a continual cursing of God. This is one of the things the Scriptures mean when they speak of souls in hell "gnashing their teeth."

And it doesn't stop there. Many other comforts that we take for granted in life are incompatible with the hellish choice to reject God. For instance, *rest*, *peace*, and *home* are all things we experience to some degree on earth, but they have their true source in God.[7] When you finish work on a Friday afternoon, enjoy a good dinner with your family, and have the whole weekend to look forward to, you can feel a certain sense of peace. But that feeling isn't just the result of having a few days off. The weekend may indeed be the trigger for some pleasant human emotions. But the reason there is a thing called peace in the first place is because there is an objective state of peace that exists *in God* and which human beings can experience *through* their emotions. Peace itself is an objective reality that comes from God.

The same is true for the concept of home. Home is not merely a human creation, a dwelling place made of wood and brick and mortar. It has a transcendent objective reality, and again, its true source is God. Your home on earth may be a mansion overlooking the sea or a one-room apartment in an impoverished section of the city. No matter how small or modest, it's still possible for it to feel like home. The reason is that home derives its power and meaning not from any locality on earth but from its objective reality in God and in heaven. That's where the good, warm, comforting feelings of home originate. Thus, if a person turns away from God, he loses the ability to feel at home or at rest or at peace *anywhere*. He is truly lost in an immense whirlpool of anxiety.

This is the existence of a soul who has freely rejected God. And it is an existence characterized chiefly by *loss*.

Now anyone who has ever experienced loss knows it can be painful. Think of how upset you get when you lose, through your own fault, a small piece of jewelry or some other possession you feel attached to. Think of how much such a trivial loss can disturb your peace of mind. What then must be the agony of someone in hell who has lost the immensity of the almighty God through his own fault?

Or think about the times in your life when you lost something that truly was important. Something that was genuinely good or true or beautiful. For instance, have you ever lost a loved one to cancer or some other terrible disease or accident? Have you ever lost a friendship that had tremendous significance to you? Have you ever lost your home or your job or your health? How about all the time you've misspent? Maybe there was a particularly happy period in your life that is gone and will never return. How does it feel to think about those things?

Well, the souls in hell experience the spiritual equivalent of this deprivation *all the time*. And it doesn't matter one bit that they hate God. They still feel the pain of having lost him and everything that comes from him. In other words, they know they have lost goodness, truth, beauty, love, rest, peace, and home, and they know why, but they still hate God. In fact, they hate him even more because they blame him for this loss.

Yes, it's possible to feel pain because of losing someone and still dislike that person. Some people who have problematic relationships with their mothers or fathers understand this. When a parent dies, they experience great sadness, sometimes intensified by enormous guilt, but they still go on harboring negative feelings toward that parent. I'm not saying they're wrong to have those feelings, merely that it's possible to dislike someone and still be affected by their loss.

It's possible, in fact, to continue hating even when you are in the midst of feeling the pain of loss. Adolf Hitler felt tremendous anguish at the end of World War II. He fully recognized that he had lost everything and that his beloved Germany had lost everything. In his final hours, he saw all the destruction and experienced great emotional turmoil. But did this recognition of his loss cause him to feel even one iota of remorse for all the evil he had done? Did he shed one tear for the millions of men, women, and children he had killed? Did he experience even the tiniest bit of guilt? No, not according to eyewitnesses and to the written record. Indeed, the last documents he signed—drafted just hours before he killed himself to evade capture by the Russians—contain the same belligerent rants against the Jews that he had been making for decades. He blamed them for everything right up until the end. His hatred for Jews never once ebbed. His evil, hellish pride never once ebbed.

So it is with the souls damned to hell. They view God as their enemy and hate him. That is the decision they made in life and the decision that was fixed immutably at the moment of their death. They are completely aware that God is happy and that there are souls with him in heaven who are happy. They are also aware it is by their own deliberate choice that they forfeited those joys. But this knowledge, instead of causing them to experience guilt, only adds fuel to their bitter resentment of God and their overall misery at having to suffer the consequences of their choice. Basically, the souls in hell regret that things didn't go the way they planned but feel no remorse at having chosen evil over good, obstinacy over repentance.

Let's be clear about this. Some spiritual writers use the words *regret* and *remorse* interchangeably, but they are two very different things. It's possible to regret something deeply without feeling the slightest bit of remorse. Many inmates in prison regret their crimes because they got caught or acted stupidly and as a result have to suffer the consequences. There's no doubt they feel badly about what happened in their lives. But the truth is, if they could commit the same crime again with impunity, they would be only too happy to do so. In other words, they have regret but no contrition. They feel badly about what they have done, but not because of any conviction that it was an offense against God or their neighbor. Contrition always involves repentance—turning back to God in faith and trust in his mercy. The souls in hell are not contrite. They are not repentant. They are not remorseful. They experience enormous regret for their tragic situation and the circumstances that led to it—and this regret is extremely painful—but they remain eternally defiant.

What makes their situation even worse is they have nowhere to turn to alleviate this pain. On earth, when a person rejects God, it's possible to turn to other created things for solace. It's possible to turn to books, television shows, movies, work, sex, traveling, food, nature, animals, other people, and so on. The world is so full of things that reflect God's goodness that they often captivate, console, and distract us. Thus, it's possible in this life to obtain pleasure even when one has rejected the source of all pleasure.

In fact, this is what often happens when a person sins. Sinning, by definition, is the act of turning away from God. When someone sins, he may experience guilt or pain as a result of the sin, but he will also invariably experience various kinds of worldly pleasures—all of which come from God, though the sinner may not know it. Let's say, for instance, that a man commits adultery. Essentially, he has said no to God's law concerning the sanctity of marriage and human sexuality. He has turned away from his spouse and committed a sin with another woman. Eventually there is going to be pain and loss that results from his sin. If the person does not repent and change his adulterous ways, he might possibly lose his marriage, his family, his peace of mind, and even part of his income and property in the form of a costly divorce settlement.

But despite these pains of loss, he is also, presumably, deriving pleasure from the sexual relations he has with his new partner as well as pleasure from his new, illicit romance. Both human sexuality and romance are gifts from God. The man has succeeded in distorting them into sins by his improper use of them, but they themselves are of divine origin. As C. S. Lewis said in *The Screwtape Letters*, all pleasure is a creation of God. He invented it. The rightness or wrongness of a particular pleasure depends totally on the action that brings it about. When human beings sin, they take pleasures that are good in and of themselves and use them in the wrong ways, at the wrong times, or in the wrong degrees, essentially twisting them into evil actions.

Thus, a person can rob a bank and use the money he steals for a beautiful vacation to Italy, which he truly enjoys. The sin of theft might eventually result in great pain to the person, in the form of a loss of peace, self-esteem, reputation, and even liberty (if he is caught and arrested). But the wonderful feeling derived from being in Italy was still real. It was still a positive pleasure, because Italy itself—apart from the sin that made the trip possible—is still a reflection of God's beauty and the goodness of creation.

The point is this: when we sin in life, we can endure whatever pain of loss that results partly because there are so many ancillary pleasures that accompany the sin. But if a person dies in a state of open rebellion against God, and that free decision becomes fixed immutably, there will be no other pleasures in hell to fall back on. The twofold act of turning away from God—the source of all goodness, truth, beauty, and love—and leaving the earth—which is so full of pleasures that reflect God's goodness, truth, beauty, and love—results in the soul being left with nothing except the pain of loss.

This loss is experienced by the soul in many forms: isolation, loneliness, self-loathing, paranoia, anger, animosity, envy, despair, and sorrow. Sometimes when we rebel against God on earth, we get a glimpse of these terrible feelings because they are a natural consequence of sinning. But they pale in comparison to what the disembodied souls in hell feel.

How so?

Think back to a time when you felt depressed and alone. Think back to a time when you knew you had failed miserably at something and, as a result, had such low self-esteem you were almost in despair. Then imagine what that feeling would have been like if you knew your life would *never* change. Only people who have been suicidal can really understand the kind of desperate hopelessness and agony we're talking about here.

On earth, we have so many safety valves, so many ways to distract ourselves with other pleasures. We can alleviate pain with the honey of life. And we can always hope that things will get better. Hope is the great cure-all in life. But the soul in hell has no honey and no safety valve. It can neither derive pleasure from God's creation nor muster any hope for a better future. All it has is the company of the devil, the demons, the other reprobate souls, and the immense void of hell.

But this is only the beginning. The souls in hell also experience pains that differ in degree according to the evil they practiced on earth. They must endure, among other things, the torment by demons as well as other afflictions that resemble human-sense suffering. There has been a tremendous amount of theological speculation, for example, about the nature of hellfire (the mysterious phenomenon we spoke of in the previous chapter) and its ability to affect pure spirits, to restrict their activities and imprison them in some suffocating manner. But these types of pains are very obscure. They're actually much better understood in light of the subject we're going to discuss next: the Christian doctrine of the resurrection. This is the teaching that all souls—both good and evil—will someday be reunited with their bodies and spend eternity in heaven or hell as complete human beings.

It is this picture of everlasting *bodily* torment that is easiest for us to comprehend—and also most horrifying to contemplate.

Seven

Arrival in Hell

The Last Judgment

N o one knows how long the souls in heaven and hell must wait until they are finally joined together once more with their bodies on the day of the resurrection. Christ was very clear when he said that God the Father has appointed that moment and only the Father knows when it will occur.[1]

Beyond not knowing the exact date, there is another problem involved in understanding God's time frame: we have no way of knowing what time itself feels like to disembodied souls.

According to Aristotle, time is defined as the measurement of change,[2] and it's very easy on earth to measure the change that takes place in material objects and living bodies. But once human beings die and are separated from their bodies, the measurement of change becomes infinitely more difficult to conceptualize. After all, how do you measure change in a pure spirit that lives in a purely spiritual environment?

To be sure, things do change for disembodied souls. In the case of a soul in heaven, the soul really, truly experiences different kinds of joys. In the case of a soul in hell, the soul really, truly experiences different kinds of pains. So *something* involving change is happening, and therefore some version of time must exist in the afterlife, even before the resurrection. It's just impossible for us to have any idea how short or long time feels. That's one of the reasons the apostle Peter wrote: "With the Lord a day is like a thousand years, and a thousand years are like a day."[3]

Now, Peter himself died two thousand years ago, according to earth time. Does it feel to him as if he has spent two thousand years in heaven as a soul, without his flesh and his bones (some of which still exist today in Rome)? Likewise, what can we say of Judas, who rejected God and—we will assume for the sake of argument—remained impenitent two thousand years ago, hanging himself in remorseless despair? Does he feel like he has spent two thousand years in hell?

It may well be the case, but it also may be the case that both this famous saint in heaven and this infamous traitor in hell feel as if a considerably shorter time has elapsed. It's even possible they have experienced something altogether different than what we commonly associate with the passage of time. We just don't know the answer. All we can say for sure is that, at some moment appointed by God, the world will come to an end, the dead will be raised, and Peter and Judas, along with the rest of humanity, will experience what is commonly called the Last Judgment.

The Last Judgment is the event Michelangelo painted so magnificently on the wall behind the altar of the Sistine Chapel. It's quite a frightening scene, with the figure of Christ at the top center, his powerful arm raised above his head in a whirling gesture of justice, the saved ascending to heaven on his right, and the damned descending to hell on his left. One of the most striking features of the fresco is that it is so crowded with people and angels and demons and saints. In this way it is actually quite true to the imagery used in the Bible. For unlike the judgment that occurs immediately after we die, which is centered on the individual and is very much a private moment between each human soul and God, the Last Judgment is going to be *public*.[4]

We all know that when Christ came to earth the first time, two thousand years ago, he did so very quietly, in fact almost secretly. The first Christmas took place in a shabby stable, with only Mary, Joseph, a few small animals, and the silent stars as witnesses. That's not going to be the case the next time he comes. According to Scripture and Christian teaching, at the end of the world, Christ will come back in all his power and glory for everyone to see. And he's going to be here not as redeemer, teacher, or miracle worker but as the almighty Judge of the universe.

And isn't that fitting? Since humanity itself will be judged, it makes perfect sense that the one dispensing justice will be a divine person, someone both God *and* human, someone who lived a thoroughly human life and experienced all the joys and pains and problems that we do, someone who was like us in every way—except that he was without sin.

Now the nature of the judgment Christ is going to make when he comes again will not be any different from the one that was already rendered at our death. Whether we go to heaven or hell is determined the moment we die and is based on whether or not we rejected God according to the graces we were given in life. That decision is not going to change. It will be repeated and made public, but it is absolutely irrevocable.

Nor will there be any appeals from those who are sentenced. As we discussed in the chapter on particular judgment, both the blessed and the damned will be in *full agreement* with the verdict of Christ.[5] Those who are condemned to hell will *want* to go there. They will want to run as far away from the light of God and goodness as possible.

As the great Baptist preacher Charles H. Spurgeon said:

> At the last great day, not one of the condemned shall be able to deny his guilt nor the justice of the sentence. Though sent to hell, he will feel it is what he deserves. . . . There shall be an assent in every human mind to the sentence of the Christ of God; it shall flash such awful conviction into the soul of every sinner that, though he be damned, his own soul shall say, "Amen" to the condemnation.[6]

So the verdict—salvation or damnation—will not change at the Last Judgment. What will change is that, in addition to repeating this decision publicly, all the questions we have about life are going to be answered by God. All the mysteries are at last going to be solved. All the loose ends are going to be tied and all the blanks finally filled in. In the presence of Christ, who is truth itself, the truth of each person's life will be laid bare for everyone else to see.[7]

We're going to stand there in front of Christ—all the

multitudes together, all the peoples and all the nations of the world from every period of time—in a scene so dramatic and overwhelming in its immensity that no poetry or painting or metaphor or movie could possibly do it justice. And in a flash, we're going to know the truth about ourselves and the truth about each other. Christ is going to reveal to us the secret disposition of our hearts. We're going to see every detail of our lives, every good deed and every prayer and every sin we ever committed. We're also going to be shown what those actions led to. We're going to see their furthest, final consequences, not just for us, but for all those affected by them, even generations after we died. Who did they help? Who did they hurt? What good did we accomplish? What evil? How much did we fail to do? How much grace did we refuse? How much of our lives was substantive and worthwhile? How much was wasted and vain? All that we have ever thought, desired, said, done, and omitted to do—these are the kinds of things that are going to be judged.[8]

Think about your own life now. If you're like me, you've probably forgotten much of what you've said and done to cause pain to family, friends, strangers, and God. Perhaps you're keenly aware of your shortcomings. Or perhaps you're oblivious to the damage you've done. So many people today seem to be living in a fog when it comes to the evil they're doing or promoting. They go through life wearing the moral equivalent of blinders. They're so wrapped up in their own selfish desires and narcissistic pride that they fail to notice how much emotional carnage they're leaving in their wake. God may well forgive them for their sins, but that doesn't mean an accounting isn't due for every single one of them. It most certainly is—even if some of that accounting simply takes the form of a public disclosure at the Last Judgment.

The point is that God's mercy makes forgiveness and salvation possible, but justice must always be done.

On the fateful day of the Last Judgment, we're going to hear every kindhearted word we ever spoke and see how they comforted those around us. We're also going to hear every lie, curse, and mean-spirited thing that ever came out of our mouths, from the time we were children to our very last moment on earth. And we're going to be shown with brutal clarity how they helped or hurt all the people we knew.[9]

We're also going to find out the answers to questions we've asked throughout our life. Why did my mother die when I was so young? Why did my father get Alzheimer's? Why wasn't I able to have children? Why was my son killed in a car accident? Why was that child sexually abused? Why was I so lonely and depressed for so many years? Why did I lose that job when I needed it so badly? What was the meaning of all my suffering? All of these questions and more are going to be answered. On that day, the apostle John said, there will be no more questions.[10]

Essentially, the Last Judgment will provide God the opportunity to pronounce the final word on history. In one mysterious, miraculous moment of direct intuition of Christ's judgment, we will be told all the details regarding the ultimate meaning of life and creation and understand the ways by which God in his providence was able to lead everything to its final end. Everyone knows that the story of mankind on earth has often been incorrectly and even fraudulently recorded. Think of how historians, scholars, and members of the media today have purposely distorted history to suit their own moral biases and political agendas. Think of the crimes of socialism, communism, and totalitarianism. Think of the crimes of our own horrifying culture of death.

Think of how so much of this evil has been swept under the rug by those who should have known better. At the Last Judgment, all will be revealed, and humanity will know that God's justice has finally and definitively triumphed over all the terrible injustices committed by his creatures.

According to the famous Thomistic theologian Reginald Garrigou-Lagrange:

> Dead men live in the memory of men on earth and are often judged contrary to truth. . . .
>
> Judgment Day will show how much value is to be assigned to certain histories of philosophies. . . . It will manifest all lying propaganda. . . . The secrets of the hearts will be revealed. . . . Truth will conquer all these lies. It is clear that if God exists, truth must be the absolutely last word.
>
> Truth and justice must be vindicated. . . .
>
> Lastly, the effects of men's actions last long after their death. . . .
>
> Divine justice wills that the good recover their reputation, often attacked by the wicked who triumph. Further, the body, as well as the soul, must receive the punishment or the reward which it merits.[11]

Understand the important points being made here. If the personal God of Christianity exists, he is certainly a God of justice.[12] It is abundantly clear that the life we live on earth is not just. In fact, it is often cruel and unfair, not only to those who are living, but also to the memory of individuals and groups and nations who have died. Therefore, if God is not a liar or a fake, the scales of justice must be balanced at some point. And this final act of true justice, this final victory of good over evil, is what will take place at the end of earthly time.

The last point Garrigou-Lagrange makes—about the need for the body as well as the soul to receive justice—is especially key to our discussion of hell. For just before the Last Judgment, Christianity teaches that all human beings from all places and times, both righteous and unrighteous, will experience the marvel of the resurrection. In other words, they will either rise from the dead or, if they are alive at the time, their bodies will be changed in some mysterious way. The Bible refers to this bedrock doctrine of faith many times:

All flesh shall come to adore before My face.[13]

[This will be] "the hour when all who are in the tombs will hear Christ's voice and come forth, those who have done good, to the resurrection of life, and those who have done evil, to the resurrection of judgment."[14]

"But in the account of the burning bush, even Moses showed that the dead rise, for he calls the Lord 'the God of Abraham, and the God of Isaac, and the God of Jacob. He is not the God of the dead, but of the living, for to him all are alive."[15]

[Then Christ will come] "in his glory, and all the angels with him. . . . Before him will be gathered all the nations, and he will separate them one from another as a shepherd separates the sheep from the goats, and he will place the sheep at his right hand, but the goats at the left. . . . And they will go away into eternal punishment, but the righteous into eternal life."[16]

"Listen, I tell you a mystery. We will not all sleep, but we will all be changed in a flash, in the twinkling of an eye, at the last trumpet. For the trumpet will sound, the dead will be raised imperishable, and we will be changed."[17]

"For we must all be manifested before the judgment seat of Christ, that everyone may receive the proper things of the body, according as he hath done, whether it be good or evil."[18]

"And I saw the dead, great and small, standing in the presence of the throne. And the books were opened . . . and the dead were judged by those things which were written in the books, according to their works."[19]

One of the main points being conveyed in these verses is that, when the Last Judgment occurs, those who stand before Christ will have *physical bodies*. So many people have an over-spiritualized idea of the afterlife. When they imagine heaven, all they think about is the soul. They forget the body is also a magnificent creation of God and that it, too, is destined for immortality. At the end of the world, we will not just be pure spirits in heaven; we will be whole human beings once again, with bodies and souls united as they were meant to be from all eternity.

Remember, the soul is incomplete without the body, and the body is incomplete without the soul. Human beings were made by God to be *one* creation. Thus, if we go to heaven, we won't turn into angels, and if we go to hell, we won't become demons. On the day of the Last Judgment, our bodies and souls will come together again in a similar way that Christ's body and soul were reunited on the day of his resurrection—the first Easter Sunday.

Recall that Christ died a brutal death on a cross. He underwent horrible suffering and experienced bodily death in the same way you and I will. But when he rose from the dead, it wasn't just his spirit that came back to life; it was the whole person. When he appeared to his disciples, the same lungs that had gasped for air on the cross were breathing again. The same mouth that had uttered his final agonizing words was speaking again. The same muscles that were racked with pain as he hung from the wooden beams pulsated with blood and moved again. The same heart that had stopped at 3:00 p.m. on Good Friday was beating again.

And it is still beating today in heaven.

That's what's going to happen to us. On the day of the resurrection, *we're* going to be reunited with our bodies. Of course, those bodies won't be exactly the same as the ones we have right now. If we go to heaven, they're not going to be old or infirm or broken or weak. They're going to be changed and perfected and spiritualized. More accurately, they're going to be what theologians call *glorified*. That means they will have certain kinds of amazing powers that directly result from being reunited with the soul. No one knows for sure what those powers will be. But we have some idea based on what Christ's risen body was like. As the apostle Paul said, Christ represents the firstfruits of what we will be like in heaven.[20]

We know, for example, the risen human body will be so completely *synchronized* with the soul that it will be possible for it to obey anything the soul commands. Right now, the opposite is the case: "The spirit is willing, but the flesh is weak."[21] If we want to do anything significant in life, it requires a great deal of willpower to overcome all the obstacles that stand in our way and all the natural inertia that comes with being fallen human beings. But in heaven, the body will actually listen to the will of the soul without any kind of pushback, and it will have the supernatural power to do practically anything the soul wants to do. The risen body will be able to travel anywhere, at any time, instantaneously. The risen body will have the ability to live forever without getting old or weary or bored. The risen body will have the ability to experience joy and ecstasy with an intensity that would kill us if we experienced it today. Most important, the risen body will be able to see God face-to-face, as we spoke about in the previous chapter.

Indeed, the resurrection is one of the most comforting beliefs of Christianity. To know you're eventually going to have a body means that when you meet your departed friends and relatives in heaven, you're going to be able to see them *in the flesh*. It means that when you see your mother again, she won't be some kind of ghost. It will really be *her*. You'll be able to hug her and kiss her and feel the warmth of her skin and hear her voice again. That's one of the great blessings God has bestowed on us as human beings that he did not bestow on the angels. Our bodies in heaven will *add* to our eternal happiness because they will enable us to delight in both physical and spiritual realities. That combined joy is what resurrected human beings are destined to experience in heaven.

But for the souls in hell, alas, the resurrection means something quite different. They, too, will have their bodies again. And they, too, will be both immortal and incorruptible. But those bodies will not be glorified at all—quite the reverse. If people who go to heaven become more of who they were meant to be, if they actualize all the potential God envisioned when he created them and are given even greater power, then those who go to hell will become even *less* of themselves. In turning away from God, they will have completely shut themselves off from his grace, and thus even the good they might have once possessed must shrivel up and disappear. C. S. Lewis said that what is cast into hell is not really a person at all but the "remains" of a person. It's what's left after the final rebellious choice has been immutably fixed and all the good has drained out. Christ seemed to affirm this when he ominously said: "Whoever has will be given more, and they will have an abundance. Whoever does not have, even what they have will be taken from them."[22]

It's hard to imagine what these human remains will be like. We know they will possess the same unique identity they had on earth and probably the same memories. But what will these pitiable creatures look like? What kind of pain will they feel? What kind of thoughts will they think? What kind of things will they do? What will they see when they look around them in the dark caverns of hell? Those are the types of questions we're going to be exploring over the next few chapters.

A Monstrous Makeover

The Human Body in Hell

We have been following the tragic, step-by-step progress of a person who goes to hell.

We've talked about the real possibility of someone choosing evil and remaining obstinate and unrepentant in that evil, even until death. We've talked about what happens at the moment of death itself, when the human soul separates from the human body and the free choice of that person to reject God and embrace evil is fixed immutably and irrevocably. We've talked about the pain the disembodied soul experiences as it awaits the resurrection, when it is joined together once more with its body and sees all the evil choices it has made in its earthly life and all the final consequences of that evil.

But now that soul and body have been reunited in hell—immortal and incorruptible,[1] never to be separated again—it's time to discuss what happens next to this most unfortunate human being.

Christianity teaches there are various kinds of hellish suffering. The first we have already touched on and will continue to refer to throughout this book: the pain of the loss of God and all the things in creation that reflect God's goodness. This is the greatest form of suffering by far, but sometimes it is difficult for us to relate to because we are so tied down to earthly pleasures that the idea of losing God can seem a bit too abstract. There are other pains in hell, however, that are more concrete and easier for us to get our minds around. Here is a brief summary of them.

1. The person in hell experiences interior pains that come from his own reprobate body.
2. There are exterior pains that come from living in the toxic environment of hell itself.
3. There are the very real torments of the demons, the fallen angels we talked about previously.
4. There are pains associated with living with the other hateful and hideous residents of hell.
5. There are pains that result from the other so-called punishments of hell.

We'll discuss each of these afflictions, but right now we need to focus on the first one, the pain that comes from having a hellish body.

Christ used a horrific image to describe the suffering people in hell when he said, "Their worm does not die."[2] He was actually quoting the prophet Isaiah: "And they will go out and look on the dead bodies of those who rebelled against me; the worms that eat them will not die, the fire that burns them will not be quenched, and they will be loathsome to all mankind."[3]

Now this doesn't necessarily mean, of course, there are real flesh-eating worms in hell. The passage can refer to any kind of eternal pain, including the emotional regret and resentment of the damned. But it can also represent real physical pain. The inner bodily torments that humans experience in hell might very well be similar to maggots who attach themselves to a host corpse on earth.

How can something so disgusting be possible?

The best way to understand the concept of bodily suffering in hell is to simply think about what happens to you now, in this life, when your body causes you pain. Everyone knows what it's like to be sick or injured in some way and how it can make life unbearable. It doesn't matter if you have something serious, like cancer or heart disease, or if you're struggling through the side effects of medical treatments, like chemotherapy or radiation therapy, or experiencing a less-threatening ailment like gallstones or kidney stones or a toothache or a stomach virus or sciatica. The bottom line is that *anything* that causes you physical pain has the ability to ruin almost *everything* in your life.

You could be on a luxurious yacht, sailing the Mediterranean, but if you have a nasty case of the flu, you're not going to be able to enjoy the scenery or the water or the wonderful food and wine. You could be home on a weekend, ready to sit back and watch some television or read a good book, but if you have bad menstrual cramps and feel like someone with a steel-tipped boot is kicking you in the lower back and stomach, you're not going to be able to relax, no matter what you do. You could be happily in love with your wife and celebrating Christmas with your whole family, but if you have a gnawing pain in your side and you suspect it might be a tumor, you're not going to derive one iota of joy from the holiday cheer.

It's a cliché, but when you lose your health, you lose practically everything. You certainly realize how valuable your health is and just how much you take for granted in life. The simplest things, like sitting or lying down or walking or breathing or sleeping or just getting through the day, can become nightmarish experiences filled with stress and anguish and even agony. While it's true there are many things *outside* you that can cause pain—like being attacked by another person or getting into a car accident or banging your thumb with a hammer—there's no doubt you carry *within* you the greatest source of potential suffering.

It's also obvious that if you abuse your body, it's going to eventually deteriorate and become wracked with pain. If you go to fast-food restaurants all the time and never exercise, you're going to become obese and begin suffering from back and knee injuries and eventually heart problems. If you drink too much alcohol, you're going to destroy your liver. If you become a drug addict, you're going to have a whole slew of neurological problems and your body is liable to become one big sore. This is just common sense. If you abuse your body, your body is going to abuse you. It's going to subject you to an enormous amount of pain, and you won't even have to leave your home to experience it. The pain will come from inside.

And here is where the connection to hell comes in. What people don't understand is that when you rebel against God and indulge in evil, the whole person suffers, not just the soul. In fact, when you sin and do not repent, you harm your body every bit as much as your spirit. Sinning always results in disintegration and disorder of the whole human being. It's just that the price paid by the body isn't immediately visible to the eye.

This is a difficult concept to understand, but it is a theological fact nonetheless. It doesn't matter what kind of exercise routine you're doing. It doesn't matter what kind of health kick you're on. You may be going to the gym five times a week, lifting weights, running on the treadmill, taking your vitamins, and doing Pilates. You may look great and feel great, and your doctor may even tell you that you're going to live to be a hundred. But that's only part of the story. There's something invisible that your doctor is missing, and that is the connection between the body and soul. If you're embracing evil on a regular basis, your body is going to be sustaining great unseen damage.

That doesn't mean that robbing a bank or committing adultery is going to make you grow a tumor (although the stress from that kind of behavior might certainly result in health problems). Nor does it mean that if you are suffering from some kind of disease, the reason is that you or one of your ancestors grievously sinned.[4] But what it does mean is that your body—the temple of the Holy Spirit—is somehow going to be affected physically by your impenitent rejection of the Holy Spirit.[5] Think of it like this: What happens when a house is left vacant for a long period of time? Weeds grow, paint peels, windows break, wood rots, and everything starts to fall apart. The same thing happens to the human body when God stops living there. Evil starts to take root and spread through every vein and capillary. Only you don't always see the physical deterioration in this life.

But you will in the next.

I've used this example before, but it's worth repeating. In Oscar Wilde's novel *The Picture of Dorian Gray*, the main character is a corrupt but handsome young man who sells his soul to the devil in order to keep his youthful beauty. The catch is that, instead of him, a portrait he commissioned of himself must age instead. And that's exactly what happens. The young man lives a life of selfish, hedonistic debauchery, committing every sin imaginable. But though many years go by, his face and body remain unchanged. The portrait, however, begins to age. Not only that, it begins to undergo disfigurement with every sin the man commits. Before long, the painted face is hideous, with open wounds and warts, puss-filled lesions, and blotchy, scaly skin. The portrait starts to resemble a monster, which is, of course, exactly what the man has become. Every portrait attempts to capture the soul of its subject, but the one in this book truly succeeds. In fact, the appearance of the man's soul in the picture is so sickening that the man must cover it with a blanket and hide it from sight. Eventually he's so repulsed by it that he tries to destroy it. In doing so, he kills himself, and at the very moment of death, his body transforms into its true grotesque appearance, while the painting reverts to its original, pristine form.

The point of the story is that no matter how wonderful we may look on the outside, our evil actions do something to us on the inside. They cause us to have an interior ugliness that no amount of plastic surgery can alter. The story also conveys very accurately what happens to us both physically and metaphysically when we lead lives of sin. We may not be able to see any bodily effect right now. But after the resurrection, the souls in hell are doomed to rise to eternal life in their *true* forms—in those very same decrepit, grotesque, repulsive bodies they created in life. Only now those bodies will be visible for everyone to see.

How do we know? The answer goes back to that bedrock teaching of Christianity that we discussed in the previous chapter: A human being isn't just a body *with* a soul or a soul *with* a body. It is a true hybrid. It is one creature, body and soul united and destined to be one entity together, forever in either heaven or hell.[6] Whatever affects the soul affects the body and vice versa. If you kill the body, the soul must leave (at least temporarily), and if you corrupt the soul, the body is somehow corrupted and contaminated in an invisible fashion, to be revealed at the end of the world, at the resurrection.

Let's try to really understand this. Christianity teaches that, in heaven, you become the best version of yourself. All your potential is fully actualized. You become who you were really meant to be. Your glorified body, in perfect communion with God—who *is* life and beauty and order—is transformed in such a way that it becomes full of life, beauty, and order, much more than was ever possible on earth.[7]

In hell, the opposite is true. Having rejected God, both body and soul become the very essence of ugliness and disorder. Yes, the reprobate person still has some life left in him, because God created humans to be immortal. But it is not a vibrant, healthy, powerful life. Rather it is more like death in life, and it is characterized by decrepitude and weakness. Whatever that person did on earth to debase himself is now manifested in visible form. Whatever sins he indulged in are no longer hidden behind a pretty, perfect, shallow exterior.

Remember, it's possible to fool people in this life. Good and evil are so mixed up here that a person may look lovely on the surface but underneath be morally disfigured. In other words, earthly appearances can be deceiving. They don't necessarily match up with the person's real identity. Christ condemned the Pharisees for this very sin. He said they were hypocrites and called them "whitewashed tombs, which look beautiful on the outside but on the inside are full of dead men's bones and every impurity."[8]

But when a person goes to hell, there is no more mixture of good and evil. There is no earthly attractiveness to hide behind. The damned are not free to be hypocritical whitewashed tombs. Their inner ugliness cannot be masked by any kind of outer beauty, because basically *there is no beauty in hell*. In choosing hell, the person has rejected beauty and is left with nothing but his own true, hideous, sickly form.

Now the subject of beauty is a complicated one, and we will discuss it more fully in the next chapter, but in classical Christian philosophy, beauty has to do with varying degrees of perfection in both the attributes and the operation of any created thing. Since human beings in hell have chosen to turn as far away from God as possible, and since God is the source of all beauty, it follows that they will possess the *absolute minimum* amount of that quality.

Although the Bible does not specifically say there are different types of bodily ugliness and bodily suffering in hell, it does strongly indicate that judgment will be experienced quite differently for different sinners. For instance, the apostle John reported, "And I saw the dead, great and small, standing before the throne. . . . Another book was opened, which is the book of life. The dead were judged according to what they had done as recorded in the books."[9]

Indeed, the Bible speaks about comparative levels of judgment in various places.

For instance, Christ said, "Truly I tell you, it will be more bearable for Sodom and Gomorrah on the day of judgment than for that town [which had refused to receive the disciples]."[10] He added, "Woe to you, Chorazin! Woe to you, Bethsaida! For if the miracles that were performed in you had been performed in Tyre and Sidon, they would have repented long ago. . . . But it will be more bearable for Tyre and Sidon at the judgment than for you."[11] And in the book of Revelation, an angel warns: "Give her as much torment and grief as the glory and luxury she gave herself."[12]

Mainly, though, there is the example of Christ himself. When Jesus rose from the dead, his own glorified body was marked by his wounds: the nail holes in his hands and feet and the gash in his side from the spear that was thrust there by a Roman soldier. These wounds were fixed forever in the act of love in which Christ died. And since Christ represents the first-fruits of how human beings will be after their resurrections, it makes sense that the bodies of the damned would also remain fixed forever in the acts of hatred in which they died.[13]

This doesn't mean that everyone in heaven and hell will have all the scars from their past earthly injuries. They won't. In fact, their bodies will likely be restored to working order, and in the case of the blessed in heaven, they will be perfected beyond our wildest dreams. What I'm talking about here goes much deeper. When we see Christ in heaven, he will have his blessed wounds because they are part of the essence of who he is and what he lovingly sacrificed for us on earth. The bodies of those in hell will likewise be marked for eternity by the repugnant essence of who they are and what they did in rebellion against God on earth.

Thus, if a person is gluttonous, he may be able to disguise his appearance with an efficient metabolism, regular exercise, or well-tailored clothes while he lives on earth. But if he rejects God and goes to hell, his lifelong gluttony will no longer be invisible. Rather, it will be manifested, perhaps in a loathsome, repugnant, obese body that perfectly reflects the sin of gluttony, along with whatever other disorders and pains and putrefying odors accompany such a state.

In other words, there is every reason to believe the body in hell *will mirror the soul* in a strikingly appropriate way.

Take the sin of anger. A person who is hateful on earth is sometimes able to put on a phony, cheerful face and act civilly to his coworkers—and then go home and beat his wife. In hell, however, the prideful hostility in his soul will no longer be hidden. As a reprobate, his face may be forever locked in rage, his body taut and tense like piano wire, his blood throbbing with a pressure so high his head feels like exploding. This is what anger does to us on the inside. And the body in hell will show it on the outside.

Likewise for the other deadly sins. A person who is lazy and slothful on earth can try to conceal it. But the resurrected body in hell will manifest that sloth in all its gory glory. Of course, no one can say for sure how. Will the person's body appear snaillike or sluglike? Will the face be fixed in a dull expression of boredom and lethargy and fatigue? Will the accumulated pain from a lifetime of putting off necessary duties somehow be embodied in an aching, hurting, formless flesh? Who knows.

Indeed, if you have a good enough imagination, you can picture all the sins of the soul displayed as outward bodily states. Such fantastic imagery may not be exactly accurate in the end, but at least it gives us an idea of the kinds of human bodies that might exist in hell. Dante, in his *Inferno*, masterfully described many frightening possibilities. According to his poetic way of thinking, if envy is the sin that characterizes your earthly exist- ence, and you remain obstinate in it until death, then perhaps in hell your eyes will be unnaturally enlarged, without eyelids to blink, opened wide forever, always looking at everything and everyone with covetousness. If malicious lying and gossip char- acterize your impenitent earthly existence, perhaps the toxicity of your breath will cause you to perpetually choke and cough.

Of course, this is just speculation, but it is not idle, foolish speculation. If anything, the disfigurement of hellish bodies will be *more* horrible than what we've described here. That's because such conjecture is based on a solid theological truth. The soul and body will be judged by Christ *as one creation*.[14] And the out- ward appearance of the risen reprobate body, as well as the pain it suffers inwardly, will arise from the very nature of the sins it committed on earth. Disorder and perversion in the soul equal disorder and perversion in the body. Hell will literally be filled with different kinds of monstrous human beings, as many as there are different types of evil that exist on earth today.

And as we said earlier, the pains that result from this disorder will differ in degree as well. Just as a person who abuses his body only slightly on earth does not experience as much bodily pain as someone who abuses his body significantly, likewise, in hell, pains will differ in intensity according to the evil of the individ- ual. The more extreme the hatred of God on earth, the more vivid the experience of isolation, resentment, and separation from divine goodness in hell—and the more tormented the body.

For example, a person in hell whose earthly rejection of God caused him to initiate a holocaust or genocide is going to have a body that corresponds to those abominable acts, and consequently it will be far more ghastly and racked with pain than that of other, comparatively less evil people in hell. The simple rule is this: the further away from God a person is in this life, the further away he will be from beauty, order, health, happiness, and vibrancy in the next.

Now some Christians disagree with this. They think that on the day of the resurrection, the damned will get bodies back that are as good as new. Their belief is based on the idea that the human body, once unhampered by the fallen nature of the world, will return to its perfect form. They admit the bodies of the reprobates in hell will be able to suffer, of course, but they don't think those bodies will be deformed or decrepit in any way.

They sincerely believe this, but in the opinion of this author, they are sincerely wrong. Yes, the human beings in hell will have bodies that function. Yes, their physiologies will be sound. Yes, they will be immortal and incorrupt. Yes, if they had limbs that were missing or broken or wounded on earth, those limbs will probably be restored to them. But it's just impossible for the damned in hell to retain or regain anything resembling bodily beauty.

My goodness, the most beautiful thing in all creation is the human body. As Shakespeare said in *Hamlet*, "What a piece of work is man! . . . In form and moving how express and admirable! In action how like an angel, in apprehension how like a god! The beauty of the world. The paragon of animals."

Can anyone really think this kind of beauty will exist in hell, where God, the source and summit of beauty, is totally absent? Can anyone really think hell will be filled with women as beautiful as Venus and men who resemble Adonis? Of course that's preposterous. In hell, the reprobates will be deprived of all beauty as a natural consequence of their turning away from God and as a natural consequence of indulging in a life so repulsive to God.

For these reasons and more, it should be apparent that, after the loss of God, the body itself may very well be a primary source of pain in hell. Sadly, however, it will not be the only source. When the tormented creature we've been examining lifts his head and looks around him, an abundance of harrowing sights will accost his vision.

What, exactly, will he see and how will it affect him? It's time now to talk about the environment of hell.

Exploring the Terrain

What Does Hell Really Look Like?

N ow that we have found our way to this infernal place where the damned have been reunited with their bodies, we're going to start exploring the terrain. That's going to necessarily involve certain kinds of speculation, and the only way we can speculate intelligently is if we go over a little philosophy first.

Whenever we talk about hell, there's a tendency to speak in absolutes. We say, for instance, that hell is "all bad," or that hell is "nothing but pain and suffering," or that hell is "completely hideous in appearance."

It's perfectly fine to use this kind of extreme imagery, because, generally speaking, it's true. But it's not *precisely* true. If there was absolutely no good in hell, then, strictly speaking, it would not exist. This is an important philosophical point to grasp. The fact that something exists means it possesses a certain amount of goodness. We're not talking about moral goodness—good versus evil—but rather metaphysical goodness—existence versus nonexistence. In other words, if someone is alive, then that, in itself, is a blessing. That, in itself, is something positive. That's why the Bible says: "God saw all that he had made, and it was very good."[1]

Now, on a scale of metaphysical goodness, between the two extremes—God on the one hand, who is pure existence, and total nonexistence on the other—there is no end to the number of possible degrees and variations we can have. It's because those in hell have some modicum of metaphysical goodness that they are able to see and do certain things and function in some way. In other words, because they have life, they are able to live. Despite their wretchedness, they are able to operate in their environment. They are able to communicate. They are able to perceive things and know things and make choices about things. All of these abilities are part of the good of being alive. The quality of life within hell may indeed be horrible, relative to the life of the blessed in heaven or even to the people living now on earth, but it still carries with it a minimum of goodness.

Let's illustrate this idea with a very nonphilosophical example. There used to be a television show called *Prison Break*. The details of the plot are not important. The critical thing to understand is the backdrop of the prison portrayed in the series was extremely bleak. The inmates were bad men who had done bad things and were now living a miserable existence behind bars. The prison guards, too, were corrupt, and they often abused the inmates in cruel and sadistic ways. Sometimes the inmates would work together because they had a common objective, but it was always for selfish motives and always through subterfuge and lying and more criminal activity. The prison itself was gray and dingy and ugly—but not uniformly so. Some parts were drearier than others. For example, being in the prison yard was not as bad as being in the main cellblock, which wasn't as bad as being in solitary confinement. Likewise, the degree of pain and suffering experienced by the inmates was different. Thus, while prison life could truly be said to be unhappy, the inmates still had life, and so were able to experience different degrees in the quality of that life.

And here is the connection to the eternal prison of hell. The inmates there have some life left in them, too, and they also experience different levels in the quality of that life. While their existence is thoroughly miserable, it is miserable in different ways and in different degrees. In a manner of speaking, it can even be bearable—at least in comparison to the one kind of life *unbearable* to the damned: life with God.

With that understanding in mind, we can again ask the question we began this chapter with: When the damned look around them, what exactly do they see? What is the terrain of hell like?

Remember, human beings in hell have bodies of some kind—disordered, diseased, and deformed in ways that mysteriously mirror the nature of their sinful indulgences on earth. Also recall that when we are trying to get a clear sense of the horrifying vision of hell, we are not just discussing a state of mind or a state of being. We are discussing a physical reality. A *place*.

Some theologians dispute this, but orthodox Christianity has always taught that while hell might have many qualities resembling a state, it *must* have a physical component as well, at least after the resurrection of the body. Why? Because if you have a body, it follows that you will be able to move that body. And if your body can move, there obviously must be somewhere it can turn and some direction it can go. All of this points to the existence of a physical locale. If there is a physical body, there has to be a physical environment in which that body can operate. This is just common sense.

Where is the location of that physical environment? No one can say for sure. Some biblical scholars have speculated that, because there are Scriptures describing the damned as falling into an abyss,[2] hell must therefore be situated deep in the belly of the earth. Some have countered that, because evil hates good so much, hell must instead be beyond the confines of the universe, as remote as possible from the blessed in heaven. Still others have said that because the afterlife has such a spiritualized quality about it, any talk of geographic location is nonsense. The bottom line is this: no tradition within Christianity really teaches anything definitive on the subject. All we know for sure is that hell is not just a spiritual state. It will have some kind of material dimension as well.

Of course, it goes without saying that both this physical place and its physical occupants will not be of the same form or substance that we see on earth. As the Bible says, at the end of time, there will be a new heaven and a new earth.[3] Indeed, there will be a whole new creation. As we've discussed, in heaven, human beings will have glorified bodies with amazing new powers. Heaven itself will be full of new joys, new activities, new relationships, and new life. Hell, on the other hand, will be quite the opposite. It will contain the remains of life after most of the good has been drained away. As Christ said, "Whoever has will be given more, and they will have an abundance. Whoever does not have, even what they have will be taken from them."[4]

But how can you describe a place that has had all the good bled out of it? We know that those in hell have turned away from God, the source of all goodness, truth, love, joy, justice, and beauty. Therefore, the environment of hell must somehow consist in the reverse of those things: evil, lies, isolation, pain, injustice, and ugliness.

But it's very difficult to understand these terms in a practical way.

The Bible can help us, because it uses two very concrete terms to illustrate the general topography of hell: darkness and fire.[5] Let's take them one at a time.

First, darkness can signify many things. For example, it can be a metaphor for spiritual blindness. In theology, a lack of light always denotes a lack of truth. That is most certainly the case in hell. But just because hell is a place of falsehood does not mean it will not also be literally dark. According to traditional Christianity it will.

The concept of darkness actually fits in perfectly with the theological principle we just mentioned, namely, the fact that in hell there can be virtually no good because God, the source of all goodness, is absent. Well, *color* is one of life's great goods, isn't it? It is a creation of God. He made all the colors in existence, in part, to bring us joy. That's why heaven is going to be filled with color. In fact, there's no reason to believe God won't create new colors for his new creation. But if color is a positive good, then there can be practically no color at all in hell. There can be no reds or yellows or greens or oranges or purples or blues or pinks. God is the source of those colors, and God will be absent. So, in hell, those colors must be absent as well, or more precisely, they must be at an absolute minimum.

It's important to note here that the sense in which we are talking about color is neither strictly photographic nor scientific. It is *existential*. Colors are a creation of God and are manifested on earth through a process of light waves reflected through a visible light spectrum. Because of this, physicists tell us that black is not really a color but a lack of color, due to its inability to reflect light. Does that mean hell will be black? Maybe. But what we are really discussing now is the idea of colors behind the physical reality. We are talking about the very *substance* of colors, separated from material creation, the notion of colors that God had in mind even before he made the world and the sunlight through which color is reflected.

Hell will be a place without either the visible spectrum of light that we have in this life or the existential reality of colors that exist in the mind of God. This absence of color, therefore, might be thought of as darkness or blackness or some kind of drab black-and-white combination or shadowy remnant of earthly colors. Or it might be something completely beyond our ability to imagine. It might be the result of the physical location of hell in some kind of cavernous pit at the center of the earth, or it might be due to the fact that God—the source of all color—is absent. Only one thing is certain: whatever hell looks like, it will be gloomy. For a world without a genuine variety of real, vivid colors is a depressing world indeed.

None of this, of course, is meant to imply that people in hell won't be able to see. They will. The darkness of hell will not preclude vision. The damned will be in a physical place, and they will have eyes that work in some way. As noted earlier, there will not be a single moment of blindness in the afterlife. Perhaps the best way to imagine hell is to think of those eerie night-vision images we sometimes see on television. Those videos are dark and ghostly, and yet we are still able to make out all the objects and creatures on the screen. It's logical that something similar will be possible for those in hell. They will be immersed in a dismal, obscure, colorless darkness, but they will not be spared the vision of seeing the horrifying things that exist in that darkness.

This same principle can be applied to the other bodily senses, all of which will continue to operate in hell. For instance, the damned will be able to hear, but there will be no music there. Nor will there be any peaceful, lovely silence. Both of these are good things that come from God. Therefore, they will not be present in hell in any significant way. In fact, C. S. Lewis called hell a kingdom of noise. He said that noise is the "audible expression of all that is . . . ruthless."[6] Indeed, shouting, screaming, angry muttering, accusatory conversation, endless complaining, moaning, vile words, curses, blasphemies—these are the main sounds that will echo through the bleak corridors of hell.[7]

Likewise, nothing in hell will taste good or smell good or feel good. The pleasure derived from eating something delicious comes from God. The pleasure derived from smelling flowers or freshly cut grass comes from God. The pleasure of feeling the softness of a person's skin or the cool wetness of bathwater comes from God. None of these pleasures can exist in a world without God. If you want to picture hell, just imagine all the various sensory experiences that might be furthest away from the goodness of the Almighty. What kind of sights are most unpleasant? What kind of sounds are most unpleasant? What kind of smells are most unpleasant? (Think of the stench of diseased and decrepit, hellish bodies.)[8]

We'll discuss this subject more later on, but it's sufficient to say that, while the damned may still retain their ability to eat and smell and touch by virtue of having bodies, and while their gluttonous and carnal behavior may still continue by virtue of their warped wills, they will not be able to derive any *gratification* from these indulgences. They will search the landscape with eyes that function, listen hard with ears that function, eat and drink with mouths that function, inhale odors with lungs that function, and touch the surfaces of objects with hands that function, but none of this will give them any joy. No sight, no sound, no smell, no texture, and no taste in hell will have the power to provide them with any real sensual pleasure for the simple reason that pleasure cannot exist apart from God.

And what of the hellfire we read about so often in the Scriptures and in the writings of theologians?

Many have asserted that the word *fire* is used strictly as a metaphor in reference to hell, since it is the most painful thing we can imagine on earth. They even think this symbolic usage applies to fire after the resurrection, when there will certainly be physical bodies present that are capable of being burned. But surely it goes deeper than that. The word *fire* is used too many times in the Bible in too dramatic and unequivocal a fashion for it to simply be dismissed as a literary device.[9] Besides this, the consistent teaching of Christianity for two thousand years has been that hellfire is not just metaphorical but literal. How can that be?

Going back to our guiding principle—that only the most minimal amount of goodness can exist in hell—we can also apply it to the *atmosphere* of the place. If the calm, clear, balmy, and fragrant air we breathe on earth feels good to us, then the air and environment of hell cannot resemble it in any way. Indeed, it must have the opposite qualities and the opposite effect. It must be foul and putrid and even painful. Whether the fire spoken of in the Bible is meant to have an additional metaphorical component is almost irrelevant. If the very air you breathe is painful, it's painful.

Now, not even the most orthodox theologians have ever believed that the *nature* of hellfire is the same as that of earthly fire. Of course, it must be different, just as everything in the next world will be somewhat different than it is now. The critical point to note is that it won't just be a purely spiritual fire. The fire of hell can't be equated with the spiritual pain of loss or the spiritual pain of regret or the spiritual pain of loneliness or the spiritual pain of hate. It will be something totally different and *added onto* these other spiritual pains. It will be *corporeal* in character, like the anguish those in hell experience as a result of having diseased, disordered, and deformed bodies. There will be something *physically* agonizing about the very air surrounding the reprobates, which will somehow be akin to real fire.

And doesn't that make sense? If you have removed yourself from the source of all pleasure, then you're going to experience pain both on the inside and on the outside, both spiritually and physically. In fact, you will literally be engulfed in pain, just as someone can be engulfed in flames. That's how the fire of hell should be understood.

Also, difficult as it may be to comprehend, there might even be something beneficial about the fire of hell.

It is not at all incompatible with Christian theology to speculate that hellfire has a restrictive effect on reprobate humans as well as on demons. Just as a fire that breaks out in your home can severely limit your movements, so, too, might hellfire limit the movements of the damned. Thomas Aquinas believed that, in some mysterious way, hellfire has the power to bind and hinder those in hell, like paralysis or even intoxication. This idea fits perfectly with the scriptures that describe hell as a prison in which the damned are forcibly restrained.[10] Not restrained in the sense that they are prevented from leaving the confines of hell—there is no need for that because, as we've said before, the damned *want* to be there. But they are restrained in the sense that they are fettered and frustrated in their activities.

Doesn't that make sense? On earth, a person can be limited in his ability to go places not only because of physical infirmities but also because of severe weather conditions. Intense heat or bitter cold can make it impossible to do the things we want to do. Hellfire may act in the same manner. At first glance this might seem to be just another hellish punishment, and a terrible one at that. After all, being paralyzed in any way is unpleasant. But it can also be viewed in another light.

Remember, in hell, the prideful, violent inmates all hate each other. They want to lash out at all the other prideful, violent inmates. Hell is not a loving or friendly environment. It's not a calm or peaceful place. In fact, it's very much like the prison in the television series we talked about—with psychopathic criminals and serial killers and sex offenders and rival gang members constantly at odds with one another. We've all heard stories about what those prisoners do to each other when they find a way to elude their guards. In the history of the penal system, countless numbers of inmates from every time period and every country of the world have been beaten, slashed, raped, and killed by their fellow inmates.

Some scholars have theorized that the fire of hell—which causes real and intense corporeal pain—might actually serve as a kind of security system, keeping the inmates from inflicting even more pain on each other. In other words, if the residents of hell are like vicious attack dogs, hellfire might act as a sort of muzzle by restricting their aggressive behavior. Thus, what has always been conceived solely as a punishment of God might actually be another example of his wisdom.

This is just speculation, of course, but it's speculation that makes theological sense. If there is such a thing as fire in hell—as the Bible and the Christian church universally teach—here is a way to understand it that perfectly combines God's justice and mercy. Here is an orthodox way of looking at it that doesn't make God out to be some sadistic television prison warden. The real God of Christianity allows people to go to hell because they *insist* on going, but even while they are there, he limits the torments they have to suffer as a natural consequence of their free-will rebellion. As R. C. Sproul wrote: "[If] we can take any comfort in the concept of hell, we can take it in the full assurance that there will be no cruelty there. It is impossible for God to be cruel."[11]

Now, when these muzzled human reprobates look around them, through the darkness and the fire, and in the midst of all the noise and noxious odors and bitter desolation of their surroundings, what else do they perceive? It goes without saying there aren't any animals or trees or flowers or foliage in hell. All those wonderful creations of God have too much metaphysical goodness to exist in the arid landscape of hell. That kind of abundant life is meant for heaven alone.

So what more is there?

They see their fellow inmates, of course—the damned of hell—in all their myriad and monstrous shapes, sizes, and sinful incarnations. But they see something else too: they see their new *masters*. For as the reprobates were slaves to sin on earth, so, too, now and forever, they are doomed to be slaves in hell. Not just to their own depraved wills, but to those purely spiritual creatures who inhabited hell long before they arrived, from the time of the first lightning fall from grace eons ago.

Yes, when the damned in hell look around them, they will see staring straight into their eyes the fallen angels known as demons. And among this horrid and unholy congregation, they see the most infamous demon of all.

ten

Activities in Hell: Part I

Enslavement to the Demons

What do demons look like?

In describing the end of the world, the book of Revelation says that when the fifth angel blows his trumpet, a great, smoking, furnace-like pit known as the "abyss" will open, and a horde of demonic locusts with the power to sting like scorpions will rise out of it and torture all those who do not bear the seal of God.[1]

This is symbolic language, of course, for the book of Revelation is written in the form of a prophetic dream of the apostle John. No one really believes that demons look like locusts or scorpions. In fact, there really isn't much in the way of physical descriptions of either the devil or the demons anywhere in

Scripture. And there is good reason for this. Demons, as we said earlier, are *pure spirits*. By definition, they are nonphysical and possess neither faces nor bodies nor anything material on which we might base physical descriptions. It's true, at certain times, they've had the power to assume shapes visible to the human eye, but that's really only an illusion. In their nature, they are totally noncorporeal.

Yet the world's great literature is filled with highly detailed descriptions of these pure spirits. In his epic poem *The Inferno*, Dante portrays the devil as a grotesque, hulking monster with three faces, each slowly chewing on an infamous sinner. His gargantuan, bat-like wings steadily blow freezing cold winds throughout the nine circles of hell, causing him to remain frozen at the bottom of hell forever.

Again, such horrific descriptions are not meant to be taken literally. But that doesn't mean they don't contain a good deal of truth. The book of Revelation's representation of demons as a swarm of locusts conveys the truth that the number of demons is legion and they are repulsive, aggressive, and harmful to human beings. Dante's eerie depiction of the devil conveys the idea of a massive, immovable evil that feeds on human beings, slowly grinding them up and mutilating them. His description of physical wings, which are used by the devil, not to escape hell, but rather to freeze himself into place, illustrates a concept already familiar to us: demons and humans go to hell because of their own free, cold, immutable choice.

Putting symbolic truth aside, though, it's accurate to say that demons don't look like anything, at least nothing we can compare them to on earth. There is one thing about their appearance, however, that we can say with certitude: if God is the source of all beauty, and there is an absolute minimum of beauty in hell, then at the very least, the *presence* of demons must be hideously ugly and repulsive. Indeed, it must be the very opposite of beautiful.

Somehow this *ugliness of being* must be made manifest in some way to the humans who live in hell. How that manifestation takes place we can't say for sure. Will demons only be known to human reprobates through their abusive actions? Will humans simply sense their demonic presence? Will the demons show themselves in some discernable form, as they've done in the past?[2] After all, wouldn't it make sense they would want to employ visual pain among all the tools available to them?

The bottom line is that demons *do* wish to inflict pain on human beings. In a manner of speaking, it's true they are the *slave masters* of hell. We're going to come back to this point shortly and discuss their sadistic role more fully, but let's first talk about the concept of slavery and the profound connection between slavery and humanity.

Slavery has been around for as long as written records have been kept and probably well before then. Almost every culture on this planet has practiced slavery at one time or another. The ancient Greeks, the Romans, the Egyptians, the Aztecs, the Incas, the Ottomans, the Europeans, the Africans, the Americans, Middle Easterners, and the Russians all practiced slavery for hundreds of years. More recently, Hitler and Stalin and the other totalitarian dictators of the twentieth century enslaved millions of people in labor camps, concentration camps, and gulags. Indeed, the slave trade continues to this day in the form of sex trafficking and forced child labor. Moreover, the operating principle of slavery is alive and well in the widespread institution of abortion—in which vast populations of unborn children are defined as disposable property and devoid of human rights.

The undeniable fact is that slavery is in our DNA. It's part of who we are, or at least who we became after the fall of Adam and Eve. Economics aside, the main reason for this is our own warped desire to exert ourselves over one another, to impose our wills on one another. Machiavelli talked about this in terms of the fear necessary to rule well. Nietzsche talked about it in terms of the strength of will to be supermen. Social Darwinists talked about it by invoking the phrase "survival of the fittest." But no matter what approach you take—political, sociological, philosophical, or theological—the why of slavery always comes down to one word: *power.*

Human beings lust for power. We see this lust all around us today, even though it's not usually connected to slavery, *per se.* We see it in the abusive behavior of some people toward their spouses. We see it in the tyranny of government bureaucrats, in the arrogance and rudeness of some airport officials, traffic cops, and workplace bosses. In anyone, really, who has an insecure, bullying mentality and who manages to get absolute authority in some tiny corner of the universe.

Perhaps you've felt this power lust yourself? Perhaps you've felt that terrible little twinge of pleasure when you know you have authority over someone and you exercise that authority, especially when that person has to take it or, even better, is a bit afraid of you. "Power is the ultimate aphrodisiac," Henry Kissinger said in the early 1970s. That doesn't mean power is always bad. It can be good and even necessary, especially when it's employed in the right cause and by someone with humility. But all too often that's not the case. All too often power is exercised principally because of pride and a selfish desire for significance.

Lust for power is actually the opposite of the Christian virtue of love. Love is the sacrificial giving away of one's self for the good of another.[3] Prideful power—the kind that lies at the heart of slavery and all other forms of abuse—involves sacrificing the good of the other for the perceived benefit of one's self.

But the connection between humanity and slavery isn't just due to the fact that some individuals want to dominate others. The reverse is also true. Some people have an unspoken desire to be controlled. They prefer to be told what to do. They prefer to be relieved of whatever responsibility they have to act firmly or morally or honorably or bravely. Sometimes these individuals are submissive by nature and dislike conflict. But at other times they're just too cowardly to stand up for what's right and to fight against evil. Whatever the case, these folks go through life as veritable slaves. These are the tepid, anemic souls who Nietzsche held in such contempt, the ones whose excuse for inaction is always that they are "just following orders," the ones who make the Hitlers and the Stalins of the world possible.

And there's another kind of slavery as well, one that is even more prevalent today: the slavery of people to various kinds of behavior. Think about it. People are slaves to their jobs, their schedules, their social calendars, their cell phones, their fad diets, and their favorite sins. Christ said that whoever sins becomes a slave to sin.[4] And how true that is. People who lie often become habitual liars. People who steal often become habitual thieves. People who commit adultery often become habitual cheaters. When immorality gets a grip on you, it always tries to make a slave of you.

Look at all the bad habits and compulsive behaviors that are so rampant in society today. Some of them are sinful and some are not, but all of them are addictive in some fashion. People are slaves to cigarettes and marijuana and vaping and alcohol and foods and drugs and pornography and promiscuity and laziness and status symbols. They're slaves to Facebook and Instagram and Twitter and YouTube. They're slaves to the whole vain, self-absorbed, self-centered, fame-fixated, social media–driven civilization in which we live.

Humans love to extol the virtues and glories of freedom, but the truth is that most people are not free at all. Between the obnoxious, power-hungry bullies on one side, the weak-willed, cowardly sheep on the other, and the vast, vacillating, addicted population in between, we are literally engulfed in a culture of slavery.

It's important to recognize this great illusion of freedom that exists, because it will help us to understand an essential dynamic of hell. The Bible says, "The truth will set you free."[5] Well, God *is* the truth. Therefore, as you move further and further away from him, not only does your environment become more filled with lies but it also becomes more filled with bondage. On earth, we can fight against slavery with the help of God's grace. But that won't always be the case. The fact is, for those who are damned, slavery does not end with this life. It continues forever. Indeed, slavery on earth is just a foretaste, a dim intimation of an even greater slavery in hell. Unlike heaven, which is governed by the law of love, life in hell will always be characterized by the ruthless subjugation of the weak by the strong, the submissive by the dominant, the slaves by the masters.

And it is the demons who are by far the strongest creatures in hell. Remember, demons are fallen angels; they are purely spiritual creatures with intelligence, will, freedom, and the ability to take action, including destructive action. They are real beings. They are not mere literary devices. They are *alive*. They are *immortal*. Moreover, they have distinctive personalities or "demonalities," to be more accurate. They are not all the same. They vary in their capabilities, their interests, their levels of evil, their types of evil, and their powers.

Scripture tells us that God created the demons to be good, but they became evil through their own fault, through a free choice they made to rebel against God. Yet even though they rebelled, God allowed them to maintain their various abilities in a similar way that God allows human beings today to continue rebelling against him and even commit profoundly evil crimes without striking them dead. Our God is a God of freedom. Therefore, demons still possess great strength now and will continue to do so after the resurrection of the dead in hell. They will always be far stronger than human beings in their intellect, will, hatred, and supernatural power. That's just their nature as fallen angels.[6]

And they will use that power against the reprobate humans in hell. Why? Because it's part of who they are. It's the logical result of their irrevocable choice to rebel against God. Recall the story of the fall of the demons. Christian tradition teaches that Satan—or Lucifer as he is also known—was the most powerful and brilliant of God's angels. His clear superiority was recognized by all. His brightness of being was so great that his very name means "bearer of light" or "morning star."

But this superiority became threatened. Theologians have long speculated that even at this early point in the history of creation, some hint of God's overall plan was revealed to the angels. It was made known to them that after the creation and fall of human beings, God would come into the world, empty himself, and take a human form, in the person of Jesus Christ. The angels were not able to understand the divine plan in its entirety because that would not become clear till after Christ had accomplished his mission. But the very *idea* that God would become a human—essentially elevating humanity over the angels, over even Satan himself—was too much for Satan and his followers to bear. Their pride could not take the *humiliation* of being made lower in the hierarchy of creation. They wanted to continue to be the center of that creation, the first in the order of all created beings. So they refused to follow God's will. That is why they said (like the Israelites later on) *non serviam*, "I will not serve."[7] And that is why Milton, in his epic poem *Paradise Lost*, put the famous fictional words into Satan's mouth: "Better to reign in Hell, then serve in Heav'n."[8]

Pride was therefore the principle reason for the demons' rebellion against God.[9] They wanted to *dominate*, and that desire continues to be their main motivation today. Defeated by God, Satan and his fellow demons endeavor to fight, defeat, and subject God's followers.[10] Starting with our first parents, Adam and Eve, and right up to the present times, demons have attempted to enslave human beings by enticing them to obey *their* will rather than God's.

This domination accomplishes two purposes. First, the very act of enslaving human beings satisfies their desire to be first, to thwart God's plans to elevate human beings to share in his divine life. Second, because God loves human beings, it offends and hurts him when humans are made captive.

The desire to offend and hurt God is always uppermost in

the minds of the demons, because they blame him for offending and hurting *them*. And as we noted earlier, since they can't do anything to hurt an all-powerful God, they do the next best thing: they hurt those creatures who bear the image and likeness of God.

This very same dynamic will continue in hell after the resurrection. The demons will exercise their hatred of God by tormenting the damned. They will use their greater power to inflict as much suffering as they can on those made in the image of God, those whose fleshy forms—though deformed and decrepit—still bear some resemblance to that of Christ's. And though they won't experience any true pleasure from this enslavement, in the sense of feeling a positive joy or thrill, they will certainly experience a gratification of their desire, and in that twisted way will come as close as they ever can to pleasure.

It's hard for us to imagine this feeling, because on earth, even when we do something wickedly sinful, there is usually some genuine pleasure mixed in with the sin, sometimes even extreme pleasure. It's hard to conceive of a place where all pleasure is absent. But think of the times in your life when you've been really angry, so angry that you yelled or banged your fist on a table or kicked a wall. Those actions could hardly be called pleasurable. And yet they were a direct result of the anger you felt, and they did give you some sort of release from the negative emotions you were experiencing. This is not a perfect analogy, but it's at least similar to how the devil and his demons feel when they inflict pain and punishment on the weaker human reprobates in hell. Their raw, sadistic actions satisfy their hatred to some degree, and their efforts to force humans to obey their will satisfies their pride to some degree.

Now don't misunderstand: the devil and the demons can't

truly be compared to slave masters or prison guards who are happy in their work, because *they* are serving out an eternal sentence in prison too. They are subject to the same Last Judgment at the end of time that we are; they must suffer the same torments, the same pain of loss, the same hopelessness, the same self-centered isolation. They, too, must contend with some form of spiritualized hellfire. In fact, because they are more intelligent and powerful than human beings, they are able to realize with more biting clarity just how much they have given up by rejecting God, so their suffering is even more intense.

The point is this: *everyone* in hell is miserable. It's just that the demons, by virtue of their stronger nature, are able to act as instruments of pain more effectively than human beings and are able to live out the prevalent slave culture more in the capacity of dominant masters.

With that understanding, what, exactly, will be the nature of this demonic enslavement?

First, the very *presence* of the demons will cause the human beings in hell to feel the pain of bondage. People who go to hell don't want to be close to anyone. They have rejected God and rejected love. They have chosen instead a radical form of selfishness. Their true desire is to be alone. Indeed, hell does give them some measure of the detachment they crave. They are much more isolated in hell than they would ever be in heaven. The whole joy of heaven comes from being with God, from being with the angels, from being with family and friends, together in paradise. While retaining their individuality, the blessed in heaven share a much more profound intimacy with other creatures and with God than they ever had on earth. It is precisely this kind of togetherness that the damned find loathsome.

And yet their isolation in hell—despite their wishes—will not be perfect. It will be continually interrupted. No matter how hard they tried to escape connection with other creatures in life, they will be unable to avoid the company of other creatures in hell, both their fellow human beings and the demons. We're going to talk about this forced interaction among the residents of hell in the next few chapters, but for now let's try to understand the concept.

What we're saying here is that in hell, it is a form of enslavement just to be in the horrible *company* of Satan. Imagine for a moment the plight of poor children who have to live in the same house with violent, alcoholic, drug-addicted, or sexually abusive fathers. What must it be like for them? They have nowhere to turn, no place to escape. They are forced to live under the same roof with someone whose very presence is toxic and oppressive. They are forced to watch someone who has complete authority over them act in a degrading, repulsive, and destructive manner day in and day out. Any physical harm they incur is merely added onto the general misery of their existence, the general suffering they experience just by virtue of their close, physical association with their depraved fathers.

The same is true in hell, only much worse. The humans there have a father too—the father of all lies, the father of all murders, the father of all sins. He is their true adoptive parent, and he is worse than any alcoholic or heroin addict or child molester who ever lived.

Like abusive fathers, the devil and his demons will torment the humans in hell with verbal, mental, and physical abuse. They will force the humans, through their superior powers, to do anything they command. Just read the Gospels and see all the examples of demons using their spiritual powers to inflict real harm on people. When Christ walked the earth, he rescued some of these poor folks who had been in the grip of evil for years. Christ was sent, after all, to "proclaim liberty to the captives."[11] So he continually stopped the devil from enslaving and punishing and possessing the Jews he met in Palestine. But Christ won't be in hell to stop the abuse of the humans there. The vicious activity of the devil and his demons will go unbridled and unchecked forever.

This is no joke! The devil is a cruel taskmaster! Just look what he does to people on earth now. Look how he tempts them and tricks them and humiliates them and punishes them and makes their lives a living hell. Look at all the lives he destroys through different kinds of sins and compulsions. Do you think his abusive behavior is just going to stop cold in the next life? If Satan is able to do so much now, when we still have God's help available to us through the power of grace, just imagine how much more he'll be able to abuse us when we are on his "home turf" and when all access to grace is gone.

Yes, that's what the damned will have to contend with. Aside from the pain of loss, the pain from their toxic bodies, and the pain from the fiery atmosphere in which they live, they will have to endure a new and hellish culture of slavery as well. Even worse, this slavery will just be a backdrop for even more suffering.

What more suffering could there be? We have yet to address two of the main activities of hell: the relationship of humans with their fellow reprobates and the so-called punishments they must undergo for the sins they committed on earth. Both of these are fascinating in their implications, but the second is perhaps more dreadful to imagine, for it was these punishments that Dante described with so much revulsion in his *Inferno*. Keeping in mind the poetic and metaphoric content of that work, let's dip into it briefly to experience some of its horror and draw out some of its truth.

eleven

Activities in Hell: Part II

Punishments to Fit the Crime

H ell, as we've said, can best be defined as the state and place of eternal separation and self-exclusion from God, in whom alone we can possess the happiness we desire so much and for which we were made. It's important to keep this definition in mind, because in the next few pages we're going to discuss some other kinds of hellish suffering, and we don't want to get so caught up in the gruesome possibilities that we forget that the loss of God is still the chief pain of the reprobates.

But what other suffering can there be? Isn't what we've already described enough? The short answer is no. And this is where some people begin to lose faith in the traditional Christian teaching on hell, because they think it's too harsh.

Remember, the act of final impenitence—deciding not to be sorry for your sins and turn to God in faith, even up to and including the last moment of life—is what results in the permanent loss of God. Ultimately, it is this loss of God, who is infinitely good, that makes the pains of hell so infinitely terrible. That point is not so difficult to understand once you accept the fact that people *can* choose evil over good. It's not even that hard to grasp that if you turn away from God and essentially run in the other direction, you're not only going to lose God, but you're going to lose everything that God is and represents. Indeed, you're going to end up in a place where you experience all the things that are opposite of God. We've said this so many times in this book because it's so important. If the personal trinitarian God of Christianity is identified with light, beauty, truth, family, fullness of life, love, order, freedom, and happiness, it's a simple and logical step to conceive of hell as being full of darkness, ugliness, lies, isolation, emptiness, hatred, disorder, slavery, and pain.

Again, this is just common sense. And yet hell is more than just a collection of characteristics antithetical to God. There are additional pains, and we have to try to understand them as well.

We've all heard it said that God is merciful and just,[1] but not everyone understands the simplicity of this teaching. One of the things it means is that there is a definite period of time for God's mercy and a definite period of time for God's justice. For the most part, the time for God's mercy is *now*, while we are still living on planet Earth. No matter how many times we sin and no matter how terrible the sins, God will always forgive us if we repent. God has placed the bar very low when it comes to forgiveness. One drop of Christ's blood is enough to wash away the sins of a billion universes. But once we die, the time for repenting will be over. In fact, the time for forgiveness, the time for grace, and the time for mercy will all come to a screeching halt. What will be left is our final decision about God—for or against him—as well as a whole lifetime of good, evil, and indifferent choices we either made or neglected to make. That will be the evidence God uses to judge us. The moment of our deaths (and the moment of our resurrections) will be the time for God's justice.

We must never forget that God is a God of *perfect* justice. Scripture couldn't be clearer about this:

For thou rendersest to every man according to his work.[2]

[God] will give to each person according to what he has done.[3]

How much more severely do you think a man deserves to be punished who has trampled the Son of God under foot, who has treated as an unholy thing the blood of the covenant that sanctified him, and who has insulted the Spirit of grace?[4]

Then He will say to those on His left, "Depart from Me, you who are cursed, into the eternal fire prepared for the devil and his angels. For I was hungry and you gave me nothing to eat, I was thirsty and you gave me nothing to drink, I was a stranger and you did not invite me in, I needed clothes and you did not clothe me, I was sick and in prison and you did not look after me." They also will answer, "Lord, when did we see you hungry or thirsty or a stranger or needing clothes or sick or in prison, and did not help you?" He will reply, "Truly I tell you, whatever you did not do for one of the least of these,

you did not do for me." Then they will go away to eternal
punishment, but the righteous to eternal life.[5]

What is being said in these passages? First, that everything
human beings do in life has meaning and will be remembered
by God. Second, that if someone remains pridefully unrepentant
and goes to hell, his punishments will be proportional to his
crimes.

We spoke about this concept when we discussed the kind of
risen bodies the reprobates will have. We said the graver a person's sins in life, the more decrepit and deformed his body will
be in hell. That principle applies not just to the body, though.
It applies to everything—to the amount of resentment, isolation, desolation, and emptiness that person will feel and to the
intensity of the suffering he must endure from *outside* sources—
including his enslavement to the demons, the hellfire he must
tolerate, and the humiliation of the activities in which he must
partake.

This last detail is where people sometimes get tripped up. It
concerns the various punishments that are *specific* to an individual in hell. The word *punishment* is probably the source of the
problem. Punishment in hell is not exactly the same thing as
punishment in this life. When we talk about earthly punishment,
we mean the infliction of some kind of penalty in retribution for
an offense. The penalty can serve the purpose of reforming the
offender or simply taking revenge on him.

But God's perfect justice does not consist in either of these
two aims. First, there is no possibility of reforming a person in
hell. His or her decision against God has been fixed permanently
and irrevocably, and there is nothing that anyone can do about

it. Second, in regard to vengeance, while it's true that, strictly speaking, a person who rejects an infinite God deserves an infinite punishment (as Augustine, Aquinas, and other theologians have argued), God doesn't need to "get even" with anyone. If he did, he certainly wouldn't inflict specific *everlasting* punishments on specific *temporal* offenses. That wouldn't be perfect justice; it would be an act of cruelty.

No, the meaning of punishment in hell goes deeper than this. It has to do, once again, with the free, fixed decision of the sinner. In the same way a person can freely choose evil and therefore choose to be in hell forever, he can also freely choose his own particular form of hellish activity and indulge in that forever. These activities are what we generally call the *just punishments of the reprobates*. And they may indeed seem to be great punitive measures to us but not to those in hell.

How can this be the case? Let's try to understand.

First, if you end up going to hell, you're not going to be the same person you are now. Yes, you will have the same soul, the same memory, the same basic identity. But you will have transformed yourself—through all your sinful, impenitent choices—into the worst possible version of yourself, into a hellish creature that manifests those evil choices physically and spiritually through the cravings of your will and actions. Just as your fundamental choice against God will become fixed, so, too, will your other sinful choices. In life, you busied yourself with turning into something monstrous; in hell, that work will have been completed. The result is that your very desires will be warped when compared to those of other men and women.

It all comes down to taking Christ's words more seriously. In the gospel of Matthew, he said: "Ask and it will be given to you; seek and you will find; knock and the door will be opened to you. For everyone who asks receives; the one who seeks finds; and to the one who knocks, the door will be opened."[6]

Well, people in hell spent their whole lives on earth asking for something, seeking something, and knocking at a particular door. In hell, they finally achieve their objective. They get what they were asking for. The fact that what they desire appears to us to be a punishment is only because we still have good inside of us, we are still able to look at things from a godly perspective. They cannot. They have been drained of their goodness. To them their hellish punishment is the fulfillment of a lifelong request, the attainment of a long-sought-after goal, the result of a free choice.

In other words, when people go to hell, all their lusts and corrupt, uncontrolled desires go to hell with them. And these desires only exacerbate the general suffering of hell, because they can no longer be gratified. You see, on earth—with its mixture of good and evil, temptation and grace—all our unruly passions are a source of conflict and turmoil, but in hell, they will be turned loose and given full reign because hell is the native, fertile soil for such sins. And because God is basically absent in hell—and he alone is the source of all pleasure—there won't be any corresponding comfort or enjoyment that accompanies those sins.

So while it is true to say that God punishes those in hell "according to what they have done,"[7] in the end, what his perfect justice actually means is that the reprobates remain *captive to their sins*. Only now, these sins have been stripped of all their pleasure. God judges perfectly what those sins are, but his judgment corresponds exactly to what the reprobates want. Essentially their crimes not only fit their punishments, they *are* their punishments.

Thus, if you freely and knowingly choose to be a hypocrite

in life—to pretend to be innocent while really being quite harmful—and if you continue in this sin, day in and day out, without ever being sorry, even till your death, then part of your punishments in hell will involve the continuation, in some way, of this hypocritical activity.

Likewise, if you spent your life seeking to gratify your flesh only, without ever repenting, that is what you are going to seek to do in hell as well: fixate on your body. The only difference is that you won't be able to derive any real thrill from that pursuit. Yes, there might be some kind of sick, perverted gratification of the will, but no positive enjoyment. We see the possibility of this happening even on earth, through the phenomena of diminishing returns. People who use pornography habitually, for instance, or who act in a sexually promiscuous way, find that they soon descend a slippery slope into more and more deviant behavior, because normal sexual thoughts and activities no longer provide them with the same level of stimulation. C. S. Lewis, speaking through the fictional character of the demon Screwtape, explained how the evil choices of human beings inevitably result in this kind of dwindling satisfaction:

> Never forget that when we are dealing with any pleasure in its healthy and normal and satisfying form, we are, in a sense, on [God's] ground. I know we have won many a soul through pleasure. All the same, it is His invention, not ours. He made the pleasures: all our research so far has not enabled us to produce one. All we can do is to encourage the humans to take the pleasures which our Enemy has produced, at times, or in ways, or in degrees, which He has forbidden. Hence we always try to work away from the natural condition of any pleasure

to that in which it is least natural, least redolent of its Maker, and least pleasurable. An ever increasing craving for an ever diminishing pleasure is the formula.[8]

That says it perfectly: "An ever increasing craving for an ever diminishing pleasure is the formula." That's exactly what happens to human beings when they continually commit the same sin on earth. And this demonic formula reaches its zenith in hell, where the reprobates continue doing just what they have always wanted to do, but without any corresponding sensual thrill. Like the rich man in Hades who craved just one drop of water to cool his tongue but was not able to have it, the senses and desires of the damned in hell will all be intact but impossible to satisfy.[9]

We said that in heaven the glorified body is totally under the command of the human will, but the opposite is true in hell. There, human bodies—or what's left of them—are completely dominated by a chaotic set of antagonistic and sinful desires. The reprobates are essentially enslaved by their bodily needs. Thus, they are doomed to experience not only the pains of loss and sense common to everyone in hell but also additional torments totally unique to them, based on their particular sins.

What, exactly, are these torments?

That's really a matter of speculation. With the help of the imagination, it's possible to invent some interesting "punishments that fit the crime," as the saying goes, but it's difficult to do, especially since it's so hard for us believe the reprobates really do *want* those punishments.

In *The Inferno*, Dante Alighieri goes on a frightful tour through the nine circles of hell, each the home of a more evil kind of sinner and, therefore, a more horrific form of punishment. The poet uses spectacular imagery and symbolic power to convey the idea of God's perfect justice. Since we can't compete with Dante, it might be helpful to go over some of his more striking examples, mindful of the fact that they are not meant to be taken literally, but rather exist only to illustrate the concept of just punishments.

Dante's second circle of hell, for instance, is made up of those reprobates whose primary sins in life involved lust. These men and women abandoned themselves to the storms of their passions, never learning to control their desires, despite all the damage their undisciplined actions caused to others and to themselves. In hell, Dante describes these unrepentant sinners as being swept through a massive cavern in a great whirlwind. They are doomed to abandon themselves to a spinning, tornado-like flight within the confines of the circle. They are blown forever from one end of the cavern to the other because their whole lives on earth were given over to abandoning themselves to their sensual appetites, to being blown from one carnal craving to the next. Their earthly lives, by their own choice, were a never-ending storm, a tempest of lust, and so their physical lives in hell are a similar kind of cyclone, again by their own choice.

Now, is this really the punishment for unrepented sexual sins in hell? Probably not. But that doesn't mean Dante's idea doesn't have truth behind it. In hell, the damned might very well have to partake in some kind of physical activity similar to what he imagined, because *part of their punishment will fit their crime.*

Going deeper into hell, to the third circle, are the gluttons. Dante scholar John Ciardi described the place as something resembling a gigantic garbage dump, in which "a great storm of putrefaction falls incessantly, a mixture of stinking snow and freezing rain, which forms into a vile slush. . . . The souls lie in the icy paste, swollen and obscene." And one of hell's demons—who has the form of a ravenous, three-headed dog, stands guard over the reprobates, ripping and tearing at them with his claws and teeth. In life these gluttons "made no higher use of the gifts of God than to wallow in food and drink," producers of nothing but garbage and excrement. "Here they lie through all eternity, themselves like garbage, half buried in fetid slush, while [the demon] slavers over them as they in life slavered over their food."[10]

The point again is that just as these unrepentant sinners acted like gluttonous swine in life, so now they act that way in hell. Their undisciplined, animallike behavior on earth carries over into the next world, where they howl in the dark and remain mired forever in the muck of their own filth and excess. The difference is that, in earthly life, gluttony brought them comfort, but in hell, there is no such thing as comfort. That illusory pleasure has given way to the truth of what gluttony truly is: a cold, dirty, putrid, sludge-like lethargy of body and spirit.

Throughout the poem, Dante continues to imagine how impenitent sinners are compelled to act in hell by their own iron willfulness. Thus, the angry spend eternity attacking one another, the killers submerge themselves in a pool of blood, the false flatterers are covered in excrement, which is the equivalent of their fictitious and self-serving compliments on earth. And at every step of the way, demons assist in these torments, hurling abuse at the reprobates, humiliating and driving them on with all manner of physical and verbal assaults. The damned are thus triply enslaved: (1) by their own disgusting bodies, (2) by their twisted, unsatisfied desires, and (3) by the demons.

We spoke of the sin of hypocrisy earlier. In the eighth circle of *The Inferno*, Dante places the impenitent hypocrites. These sinners spend their eternities walking around in long robes that resemble the religious garb worn by monks. The robes are gilded with dazzling gold and jewels on the outside, but on the inside they are weighted down with heavy lead. The heaviness is so great it causes them to moan in misery as they trudge slowly through the corridors of hell, on display for all the other damned to see. The meaning of this punishment is apparent: In life these hypocrites gave the appearance of being holy, being rich, and having great worth, but it was all an empty masquerade. In reality, they were lying the whole time. They managed to camouflage their heavy, ugly, selfish interior souls with fraudulent but beautiful exteriors. That was what they desired to do in life, and that is exactly what they get to do for all eternity.

Finally, at the bottom of hell, in the ninth circle, Dante places the traitors—traitors to family, friends, country, benefactors, and God (like Judas Iscariot). All of them are submerged in a frozen lake of ice. Why ice, when everyone usually thinks of hell in terms of fire? Because on earth, these men and women violated *trust*, which is the foundational principle of interpersonal relationships. They refused true intimacy and warmth. Indeed, they chose to renounce the strongest of all human bonds: love. In hell, however, their icy, remorseless natures finally get to express themselves fully. By being treacherous in life, these reprobates sought the cold isolation of selfishness, and that indeed is what they at last achieve.

To repeat, none of these punishments is meant to be taken literally. Dante wanted to explain hell to those who had trouble imagining it, to take a very challenging and dark reality and make it tactile. So he used his imagination in brilliant ways. But the principle Dante wanted to illustrate is consistent with traditional, orthodox Christian theology. All sinners in hell are not subject to the same torments. Each reprobate suffers a different form of punishment—or a different set of punishments—as well as a different severity of punishment based on his or her unique sins. The reason for this kind of proportional punishment is not the ancient notion of an eye for an eye. Rather, the punishing activities of those in hell arise from the nature of the sins themselves. They arise from the immutable desire of the sinner to rebel against God's laws and engage in disordered behavior, irrespective of the pain it causes them.

There is no way for us to accurately predict how these punishments will be carried out. We can only illustrate the principle behind them and do our best, like Dante, to envision the suffering that results. One thing, however, is sure: no matter how gory and gruesome we imagine the torments of hell to be, they cannot possibly rival the real thing. We simply cannot conceive of the terror of being in a world totally without God. Even in the worst possible earthly environment—even in a Nazi concentration camp or a Soviet gulag—there is always some trace of the divine. Even when forced to do the harshest labor or the most odious tasks, we can still raise our minds in prayer to heaven, consequently draw down the grace of God, and perhaps experience the peace that "transcends all understanding."[11] But that possibility does not exist in hell. Therefore, whatever punishments exist there must necessarily be more abominable than anything any poet or painter ever created.

Now at this point we are well into our tour of hell, and we've talked about many unpleasant things, but we really haven't spent any time discussing the traveling companions of the damned—the other human beings who will live in hell forever.

What will communication be like between the inmates of this eternal prison? Will there be some kind of honor among thieves or will they all be at each other's throats? Will they just engage in the punishing activities we've described above or will there be anything else to occupy their time? Let's talk for a few minutes about *relationships* in the city of the damned.

Activities in Hell: Part III

Relationships in the City of the Damned

We've been slowly trying to build up a picture of hell. At the moment it's still rather hazy and fractured, but in the next chapter we'll put the various pieces together and form a coherent whole.

Let's recap what we've got so far.

After the resurrection, humans in hell will have bodies. Those bodies, being intimately connected to their souls, will be pain-wracked in proportion to the unrepented sins they committed on earth. Hell itself will be both a state and a place. As a state, it will be characterized mostly by the loss of God and the hopeless despair caused by that loss. As a place, it will be characterized by all those traits that are the opposite of God:

darkness, deceit, malice, isolation, desolation, ugliness, and pain, including the pain of hellfire. These elements of hell will also be felt by the damned in proportion to their individual evil characters and the specific nature of their sins. Finally, hell will be a place of general enslavement to the devil and his demons, who, like sadistic prison guards, will assist in administering various punishments to human beings, again, unique and proportional to their sins on earth.

In cataloging these various features of hell, we must not lose sight of one all-important fact: the humans there are very much *alive*. They are not impersonal robots. They are not blobs of soulless flesh. They are not the walking dead or zombies or creatures so radically different from us that they are unrecognizable as human beings. On the contrary, those in hell are living men and women, distinguishable by gender and by individual physical traits. Their bodies, though hideous, still retain their fundamental identities as well as their ability to feel things, see things, and sense things. Their souls, though deprived of grace and glory, still retain their intellect, memory, and will.

Human beings in hell are thus completely aware of their state and their surroundings. All the different punishments we've spoken of take place within the framework of a conscious, living reality. This is crucial to understand. If you, for some tragic reason, end up in hell, your life there will not be some kind of shadowy, ethereal, semiconscious nightmare; it will be as real and clear and vivid and tactile as the life you're living right now. Once a human being is brought into existence by God, he or she remains immortal. Life *never* ends.

Now, there is one kind of punishment we have not yet discussed, and it is significant. It concerns the misery the damned

experience just by being in each other's detestable company.
Remember, human beings in hell have rejected love and connection. Despite their nature to be social creatures, they have
chosen, instead, a radical form of selfishness. They do not want
to be friends with anyone, certainly not with individuals as prideful as themselves. What they want is to be left alone.

To some degree they do achieve this sought-after isolation.
Nothing close to intimacy can ever exist in hell, because nothing
can ever break through the wall of iron-willed egotism that all the
reprobates possess. Such self-centeredness is part and parcel of the
fixed and irrevocable decision they have made to reject God. But
that doesn't mean that within this self-imposed quarantine they
are totally free from the presence of others. They are not.

It's possible, after all, to be alone and in a crowd at the same
time. Have you ever been to a party and noticed one or two
individuals apart from the group, in a corner by themselves,
seemingly unwilling or unable to join the group? Sometimes
these people are antisocial, sometimes they're in a bad mood,
sometimes they're just shy and insecure. Whatever the reason,
they make it clear through their body language that they want
to remain aloof. But no matter how successful they are at not
interacting, they can't escape the fact that they're surrounded by
people. Indeed, their inability to escape usually makes the experience more awkward and unpleasant for them.

Something like that dynamic exists in hell. Just as the
damned are aware of the presence of demons, so, too, are they
aware of each other. They see clearly the repulsive faces and
bodies of their fellow human beings. They know each other's
terrible sins as well (recall that sins are made public at the Last
Judgment). Think about how it must feel to be enclosed on all

sides by murderers, rapists, child molesters, thieves, hypocrites, congenital liars, traitors, egomaniacs, megalomaniacs, and practitioners of every conceivable type of perversion—all of them hopeless and bitter and resentful.[1]

Of course, it's difficult to imagine this. Perhaps if you were a criminal in a maximum-security prison, you might be able to relate to it in some way. But even then it would be hard. On earth there is always the possibility of experiencing joy and camaraderie—even in jail—because God is somehow able to pull good out of the worst situations through the power of his grace. But there is no grace in hell.

Still, it's valuable to try to think of a situation you *can* relate to. Maybe one that doesn't involve murderers and rapists, but rather people you just wouldn't want to be around. For example, are there individuals you know whose company you detest? People who are selfish most of the time? People who only call you when they need something? People who only talk about themselves? The world is full of narcissistic men and women. Perhaps some of your coworkers are that way? Or some of the people in your family?

Perhaps narcissism isn't the problem but just plain nastiness. Maybe you have a few nosy neighbors, overbearing in-laws, or bullying bosses. Do you like it when you have to spend time with these obnoxious folks? Isn't it true that the very atmosphere they create is poisonous?

Maybe you know some people who are physically repugnant? People who have very bad hygiene and go around with atrocious body odor or bad breath. Is it nice to be in close quarters with them, no matter how friendly a person you happen to be?

And what about when you're in a bad mood to begin with? What about when you're depressed or anxious or just stressed out? How does it feel at *those* times to have to be with people you don't like? It's tough, isn't it? In fact, it can feel like hell.

Well, that's the way hell *does* feel. Only much worse. Just as a prisoner can find some joy in jail due to the action of God's grace, so, too, the most irksome social engagement can be an opportunity for pleasure because of the good that exists in people, even the most unpleasant people. But in hell there won't be any mixture of good and evil. Everyone there will be bad to the core. The crowd of reprobates will be of a pure, distilled malevolence, and that doesn't make for agreeable company.

Hitler isn't going to enjoy being with Stalin. Osama bin Laden isn't going to like spending time with Mao Zedong. The Aztecs who practiced ritual child sacrifice in the fourteenth century aren't going to get along with the abortionists who practice infanticide in the twenty-first century. Assuming these horrid human beings go to hell (and we can't be absolutely sure), they are not going to relish each other's company. They're not going to compare notes and laugh about their mutual bond of evil. There's not going to be some phony Hollywood honor among thieves. The nature of radical selfishness is to be in competition. When very prideful people mix together, there isn't ever harmony and peace; there's usually a great deal of tension, hostility, and sometimes outright war.

One megalomaniac in hell can't love another. One bully in hell can't love another. Yes, they can work together sometimes— and we'll talk about that in a moment—but the essence of their relationship must be one of rivalry. It must involve a struggle for power. If that weren't the case, they wouldn't be in hell to begin with. That's why the relationships between humans in hell will be similar to the relationships between humans and demons. There will always be a slave–master dynamic in play, with the stronger creature continually trying to dominate the weaker.

This picture of inmates fighting each other for all eternity might seem unrealistic to some. After all, what could these reprobates hope to get out of each other? For what purpose would they try to be dominant or powerful? What possible gain is there in a world without hope?

No one can say for certain, but as we mentioned in an earlier chapter, the satisfaction of pride is the closest thing to pleasure the people in hell ever get. Gratifying their hatred by attempting to dominate others is essentially an exercise of self-love. It's really the only thing they can do to release their resentment and bitterness. Think about the times in your own life when you've been furious about something. Maybe a person at work upset you. Maybe your plans for the weekend were upset. Maybe another driver cut you off in traffic. All of us have experienced bouts of barely controlled rage. But did you ever come home and take that anger out on your family? Did you ever yell at your spouse or your children, not so much because they did anything terribly wrong, but simply because you needed to release your frustration?

Well, what you may have euphemistically called "venting" or "losing your temper" was really an exertion of your will over others whom you perceived as weaker than yourself in an effort to express your uncontrolled and misguided emotions. Abusing others—whether verbally or physically—is always about the elevation and gratification of the *self*.

This is similar to what motivates people in hell to try to

dominate those around them. The reprobates are filled with hatred for God. They blame him for all their misfortunes. They think he has wronged them and destroyed their lives. But like the demons, there is nothing they can do to hurt God. So they do the next best thing. They try to hurt others. They try to make themselves more significant by demonstrating their superiority over their rival inmates. They release some of their self-inflicted pain by inflicting pain on whoever is weaker. Hatred of God necessarily leads to hatred of neighbor—those who bear the image of God.

As we've noted, to understand hell, you really have to understand the nature of the slave mentality. Sometimes love and slavery can be confused with each other because, on the surface, they both involve the act of giving in to another, the act of relinquishing power to another. Thus, if someone loves you, you might be prone to do what that person wants. If someone hates you and has power over you, you might be prone to do what that person wants. Obviously, while the outcome of both scenarios is the same, the motivations are completely different.

Love involves *surrender*, which means sacrificing your will in selfless trust for someone else. This is what God did for us in giving the world his Son, Jesus Christ. And it's what Christians are called to do every day for each other.[2] Slavery, on the other hand, involves not surrender but *submission*: the forced coercion of a superior will over an inferior will. That is what Satan tries to do to human beings by tempting them to sin. That's also the kind of slavery that continues for all eternity in hell. Whether it takes the form of demons asserting supremacy over human beings or human beings asserting supremacy over one another, the key to understanding relationships in hell is that they involve the attempt to orient one's whole existence to the self at the expense of other selves.

This concept is relatively easy to grasp since we see a similar dynamic at work around us. However, there's another aspect to hellish relationships that's more mysterious. We said a moment ago that there was no such thing as honor among thieves in hell. That's very true. The reprobates' choice for radical selfishness precludes anything resembling real human friendships in hell. But that doesn't mean there can't be *some* cooperation among the damned.

Let's remind ourselves of a philosophical principle we touched on earlier having to do with the fact that there is a minimum amount of goodness in hell. Thomas Aquinas, building on the thinking of Aristotle before him, believed that as long as life is present, there can be no such thing as a total deprivation of goodness. The reason is that life itself is good. No matter how hideous or depraved or terrible that life might be, it always possesses *some* degree of goodness. If there were absolutely no goodness left, there wouldn't be any life left—just nonexistence.

Again, we're not talking about moral goodness, which has to do with following the commandments, repenting of our sins, loving one another, and so on, but rather of metaphysical goodness. This is the *intrinsic* good of the thing itself, the good it has by virtue of its existence.

Now, human beings in hell have existence. They live and move and have their being by the power of God.[3] There's no getting away from that fact. God gave existence to them when he created them, and once that gift has been given, it can never be taken away. No matter how low a human being sinks—even to the lowest depths of hell—he has at least the minimum amount of metaphysical goodness. One step lower would mean annihilation. And God does *not* annihilate any creation that bears his image and likeness, despite what some may claim.[4]

You can think of minimum goodness in terms of a house. If a child is mad at his father, he can try to go as far away as possible from him. Perhaps he might even run down to the basement. That basement may be dismal, dark, scary, and far from the brightness and warmth of the living room and the rest of the home, but it is *still* part of his father's house. Likewise, the damned in hell are utterly estranged from God and hence are as remote as possible from heaven, God's home. They have fled to the dark bowels and abysses of creation, but they are still *part* of creation, and therefore some of the goodness of creation is minimally and mysteriously present to them.

What does all this mean in practical terms?

Simply this: If a creature possesses the good of existence, then he has the ability to utilize that existence—even in hell. His operation within his environment may be incredibly disordered, but he still has the *capacity* to operate. If he didn't have this capacity, he wouldn't be alive. People tend to think of hell as a gigantic torture chamber in which everyone is chained down and subjected to continuous beatings or boilings or waterboardings or some other barbaric form of torture, making any other kind of life impossible. But the reality is quite different. God is not a cold-blooded sadist. He doesn't have to lift one finger to torture those in hell. All the suffering in hell is self-inflicted and comes as a natural result of loving evil and leaving God behind. Thus, the damned—while very much in continual pain—are not being held down and tortured. Though hellfire may restrict their activities, they are still able to live and breathe and move and think and somehow carry on with their lives.

Therefore, when it comes to relationships in hell, it's possible for a reprobate to do what he needs to do in order to function, and that includes being able to speak some measure of truth to the other reprobates, even if it's just for the purpose of complaining about their common enemy: God and the demons and other human beings. It means it's possible for a reprobate to work with another reprobate in the pursuit of some common objective. This working together could never result in true fellowship, of course, because that would require self-sacrifice and love and genuine moral goodness. But it doesn't preclude the attempt to come together in some fashion.

In book 1 of *The Republic*, Socrates asked if it's possible for a band of robbers to achieve their unjust purpose if they act unjustly toward one another. The commonsense answer is no. For a group of thieves to successfully pull off a heist, they would at least have to be honest with each other in a limited way for a limited time. That's a far cry from honor among thieves, but it's at least something. Complete injustice would make it impossible to achieve anything in a cooperative way because no one would ever be of the same mind. There would always be a state of civil war raging. The more comprehensive the injustice, the more incapable the group would be of accomplishing anything.

Life in hell will be just above this baseline of sustained warfare. There will be a minimum degree of good and therefore a minimum degree of justice. For all intents and purposes, anarchy will reign. But not total anarchy. Any *significant* effort to cooperate would necessarily be thwarted. The chief aim of any agreed-upon task would ultimately be doomed to failure, because its execution would proceed without harmony. In other words, there might be communication in hell but nothing like connection. There might be conspiracy but nothing like collaboration. There might be commonality but nothing like community.

Think about the Mafia. The Mafia is a loosely connected, loosely organized collection of racketeers, drug dealers, extortionists, and murderers. These criminals don't have any genuine love for each other. Some of them may get along in a friendly way, but just beneath the surface always lurks a seething anger and a ruthless desire to make a bigger score and to advance through the ranks, no matter who has to get hurt. If you study the mob closely, you'll see it is not truly organized in any stable way for the simple reason that its members are too argumentative, too selfish, too traitorous, and too violent to build any kind of lasting bonds. They would as soon kill each other as play cards with each other. Thus, they're more like terrorists, with each thug always looking for a way to maneuver for a higher position by ingratiating himself to those who are stronger and demeaning or killing those who are weaker. Life in the mob is all about power and intimidation, not about creation and collaboration.

Well, the mob in hell is a bit like that, only its members have much less ability to work together in a productive way, because they have much less good will.

The bottom line is this: in hell, only the most modest cooperative enterprises could ever be undertaken—perhaps the building of structures of some kind that might serve some mutual benefit—but not much else. And this is where the power of the imagination is required to fill in the blanks. Might there be bridges in hell, leading from one rocky precipice to another?

154 | Hell (a guide)

Might there be small, poorly built dwellings to give some protection against whatever elements make up that harsh environment? Might there be some attempts by the reprobates to make or devise things that could mitigate their suffering to some extent? Might there even be some sort of ghastly city of the damned or some sort of scattered collection of reprobate colonies?

It's impossible to say. We know that, in heaven, there will certainly be a city of the blessed and that those who live there will have the power to move about freely with their glorified bodies. In hell, after the resurrection, there is going to be a physical component to life, as well, and it is this physicality that makes the idea of hellish structures not only possible but, in the mind of this author, probable.

Again, as long as there is some good, some freedom, some communication, some cooperation, some desire to achieve some objective, there may be an attempt by the damned to create something. Human beings, formed in the image of God, are creators by nature. Though they may be doomed in hell to be flawed and failed creators, there is nothing in traditional Christian theology to prohibit us from believing that they might still try to make things—walls and chairs and shelters and roads and buildings. Speculation beyond this point, however, is futile—except perhaps for poets like Dante or Milton.

But all of this is still a hodgepodge of disconnected ideas. We need to try to pull the loose strands of hell together. There's also one very important question we have yet to answer: Is hell really forever? Many people refuse to believe this. They want to think and hope that hell is a place of temporary punishment or, at least, that there is some *possibility* of it ending. Yet the eternal nature of hell is a key doctrine of Christianity. How can we make sense of it? How are we to understand the whole concept of time in the afterlife? The best way, perhaps, is to discuss the complex question of eternity within the framework of a seemingly simpler question: What will a day in hell actually be like?

thirteen

A Day in Hell

On the Question of Infernal Time

Given the choice between having a discussion with an atheist who denies the existence of hell because he doesn't believe in God or a Christian who denies the existence of hell because he doesn't believe God would ever allow such a horrible place to exist, I'd prefer to talk to the atheist every time, because at least, there might be a chance he was an honest thinker. He would be wrong about his atheism, of course, but his sincerity would at least make a real discussion possible. With a Christian who denies hell, however, you are dealing with something very different. You are dealing with a person who denies the very fabric of his belief system and the very scriptures on which that belief system is based. He may be well-intentioned and empathetic and even highly intelligent, but ultimately he is still a Christian who denies his Christianity and, hence, betrays his Christianity. It sounds almost blasphemous to say this, but it's sometimes better for a person to disavow Scripture altogether than to attempt to rewrite it for the purpose of making it more merciful. In the first case, the person demonstrates a disbelief in God. In the second, he is trying to *be* God. And that's a much more insurmountable difficulty.

The problem with Christians who teach that hell isn't real, or that hell is temporary, or that hell exists in theory but in practice no one ever goes there (universalism), or that anyone who might go there is destroyed by God and isn't alive anymore (annihilationism) is they all flatly contradict the teaching of Jesus Christ. They all attempt to rewrite the Gospels.

Christ never said: "And the unrighteous will enter the house of God and be happy forever" or "The impenitent will be destroyed and exist no longer." Rather he said explicitly that there *is* a place called hell (Gehenna), that people go there, and that it is forever. In speaking about the suffering in hell, he described it as "eternal punishment,"[1] "eternal fire,"[2] "the fire [that] is not quenched,"[3] and where "the worms that eat them do not die."[4]

Of course, many of the things Jesus said during his earthly ministry can be construed in different ways. But not all of them. Certain statements he made simply preclude misinterpretation. Those having to do with hell are in that category.

That's why the apostles echoed Christ's teaching perfectly, by characterizing hell as: a "flaming fire";[5] "everlasting chains";[6] "eternal fire";[7] "the blackness of darkness for ever";[8] "the smoke of . . . torment" ascending "for ever and ever";[9] "the lake of fire and brimstone," in which the devil, the beast, and the false prophet "shall be tormented day and night, for ever and ever."[10]

And there are even more passages in the Old and New Testaments that *presuppose* the eternal nature of hell (for a listing, see the appendix).

There's just no getting away from this fact. You can try to invent your own religion and omit the notion of an everlasting hell, but you can't very well claim Christ as the founder of your faith and then change the meaning of one of Christ's central teachings. The truth is that Christ couldn't have been clearer when it came to either the existence of hell or its eternal duration. When so-called theologians write books and articles that attempt to inject more "mercy" into the words of Christ, they invariably end up going through all kinds of linguistic and intellectual gymnastics to prove their point. But in their efforts to somersault over Christ's unequivocal statements, they only reveal their own misunderstanding of mercy.

It's not merciful to force someone to do your will forever. The reprobates in hell don't want to follow God's will. They don't want to be with God at all. They don't want to be in heaven or with the blessed in heaven. Their free-will choice is to reject all that. It wouldn't be an act of mercy to disregard their wishes. C. S. Lewis said:

> In the long run the answer to all those who object to the doctrine of hell is itself a question: "What are you asking God to do?" To wipe out their past sins and, at all costs, to give them a fresh start, smoothing every difficulty and offering every miraculous help? But he has done so, on Calvary. To forgive

them? They will not be forgiven. To leave them alone? Alas,
I am afraid that is what he does.[11]

Yes, God leaves those in hell alone to the fate they really,
truly want. If a person purposely jumps down a deep well and
stubbornly stays there, you can't very well blame God if he is hurt
and alone and in the dark. You can't say that his suffering is an
unfair, punitive action. Likewise, if a person with cirrhosis of the
liver or chronic pancreatitis insists on drinking alcohol and, as
a result, experiences agonizing pain, you can't say his suffering
is a penalty inflicted on him by God. You can feel badly for the
person and try to understand the nature of his addiction, but that
doesn't change the fact that his pain was ultimately self-inflicted.
People who go to hell insist on drinking a poison called prideful
rebelliousness despite all the clear warnings that have been given
from time immemorial. Even worse, they drink it right up to the
moment they die. Thus, they carry that choice and that poison
with them into eternity and still go right on drinking it. It's not
due to any lack of God's mercy that they continue to experience
pain. Their sinful rebelliousness never stops, so their punishment
never stops. It's that simple.[12]

Those who deny the eternal nature of hell simply don't want
to accept the fact that people *do* have a choice to do evil and to
remain obstinate in that evil. Reprobates go to hell because the
alternative—being with God and doing his will—is not acceptable
to them. It's not so much that they love being in hell. They don't.
They hate it. But they *prefer* it to that which they hate even more—
namely, God and his kingdom of light. When they die, their
choice, like that of the demons, is fixed irrevocably. Those who
advocate universalism or annihilationism must ultimately deny

Christ's words, the two-thousand-year teaching tradition of the church, the concept of God's infinite justice, the reality of the devil and the demons, the story of the fall, and the existence of free will itself. Once you eliminate free will, the whole Christian faith comes crumbling to pieces. We'll be talking more about this in the last chapter of this book, but for now—and for the record—understand this point well: hell is real and it is forever.

Now, this leads us to an even more difficult topic. Truly grasping the concept of what forever is like is not quite as simple as establishing its biblical truth, because it involves the question of *time*. And time is a very thorny issue indeed.

We know God transcends time and is not subject to any of the laws of nature. We know he is not restricted by time in any way. We know that he sees all of history from all eternity. For God, there is no such thing as past or future. There is only an eternal present. As Christ (who *is* God) said, "Before Abraham was born, I AM."[13]

Thomas Aquinas said we should imagine that God is like a person standing on top of a watchtower "[embracing] in a single glance a whole caravan of passing travelers." That's the way God sees all the times of our lives—in a single glance.

However, beyond this theological principle, Christianity has always allowed plenty of intellectual leeway when it comes to understanding the nature of time. In fact, the whole subject of time and God's relation to it involves some of the most complicated and perplexing problems in metaphysics. For example, there are some who say that time is infinite, with no beginning and no end. There are others who agree that time is infinite but who say that it has a definite beginning and no end. Still others say that time is finite with both a beginning *and* an end.

Whatever time is, God's connection to it is even more problematic. Is God inside time or outside time? Or is he somehow both? Is time a creation of God's, just like the material world, or is it a different kind of creation altogether? Does God himself experience time in some way? We know that he is living in an eternal present and is not limited by time, but has he in some mystical way *entered* into time by virtue of his creation of the universe and, more significantly, by virtue of his incarnation in the person of Jesus Christ? Or has humanity, even more mysteriously, been taken up somehow into the Trinity and the timelessness of God's divinity through Christ?

Finally, even if we come to some understanding of time and God's relation to it, there is the added difficulty of understanding the concept of eternity. And here we come to another complex series of problems. For example, there is an A theory of time and a B theory of time, each of which addresses questions such as "Is eternity a timeless realm, without any succession, duration, or sequence of moments, or is it simply never-ending time, without any conclusion, but nevertheless similar to time as we usually think of it—with a continuous progression of moments from the past to the future?

It's really enough to make your head spin! In fact, even if you had the mind of Albert Einstein combined with Thomas Aquinas, and even if you spent your life devoted to this subject, you still wouldn't be able to conclusively prove any one theory of time and eternity. Logic only helps to a certain point. As long as we live in a three-dimensional universe and experience time on a moment-to-moment basis, there's simply no way we can truly know what eternity will feel like after we die.

Perhaps the simplest way of making sense of this subject

(from a Christian point of view) is to postulate there are probably two or even three different types of time. The first is what we experience in this life: solar or earth time. The second is what those who have died experience: a kind of spiritualized time. The third is the unique way God himself lives out his own divinity. We can't even label this last category as "time" because it's impossible for us to conceptualize the nature of God's life.

We can, however, get some idea of the spiritualized time of the dead. Over the centuries, Christian mystics—both Catholic and Protestant—have experienced so-called periods of ecstasy in which they claim to have been filled with the spirit of God and even in the presence of God or the angels or the blessed in heaven. During these times, they appeared to be in a trancelike state, which sometimes lasted for hours or even days. Yet when the ecstasy ended, the mystics always felt as if just moments had passed. The experience somehow took them out of bodily time and placed them into spiritualized time, which seemed to them almost like an absence of time. The euphoria they felt when in the presence of the divine "sped up" time so much that it almost "stopped the clock." Things were happening to them, for sure—in their minds and their souls—but they felt no corresponding side effects of the passage of time, no boredom or tiredness or drudgery. Sometimes we get a similar feeling ourselves when we are in the process of doing something we truly love. Time just flies by and we hardly notice it. Indeed, the act of love always seems to have the effect of speeding up time.

Might not it feel that way *all the time* for the blessed in heaven, when love itself is right there in front of them?

Contrarily, might not life feel just the opposite for the people in hell, where love is an eternity away? Then, instead of feeling the lightness and swiftness of time, they would endure only its oppressive, dense, lethargic, wearying, grinding, tedious, laborious, snail-paced burden—perhaps the way we sometimes experience time on earth when we're feeling hopeless and have to do something we hate.

Now, don't misunderstand what I'm saying. Just because spiritualized time may feel differently than earth time doesn't mean it won't exist at all. It will. The Bible indicates that time will continue after we die,[14] and that corresponds to common sense. After all (and as we discussed back in chapter 7), in one sense, time is very easy to understand: it is simply the measurement of change. In both heaven and hell, human beings will know things, think things, decide things, and do things. All that presupposes change. This will be especially true after the resurrection, when human souls are reunited with their bodies. If you have a body—whether glorified or reprobate—it is still a body, and by definition it will be able to move and act. If something can move and act, then it can change and therefore must exist in some state of time. That's just logic.

Since we can't know for sure how time will feel in hell, it's impossible to describe with accuracy any specific period of time there. Will hell feel like eternal boredom and drudgery or will some of it seem to go by quickly? Will there be something akin to days and nights and months and years or will it be just one uninterrupted span of endlessness? No one can say. However, given the fact there *will* be some kind of sequence and duration of moments in hell, it might be helpful to at least try to use our imaginations to pull together a few of the things we've been talking about in this book.

With that goal in mind, what might a day in hell look like?

First of all, you have to remember that if you were in hell, your basic state would be one of rebelliousness and despair. That's a hard thing for most of us to imagine. Can you think of a morning when you woke up and were immediately assaulted with the sensation of overwhelming stress? The knowledge you had to face all kinds of horrible problems and there was nothing you could do about it? That's one of the worst feelings in the world, to wake up and feel all that weight on your chest. If it's ever happened to you, maybe you also felt a tinge of resentment about it. *Why me?* you might have thought. It's very frustrating when you have nowhere to turn and no way to escape. No hope at all, just pain and depression.

Imagine having that state of mind and then having to also contend with serious bodily ailments: back pain, head pain, joint pain, knee pain, stomach pain. Perhaps even worse, pain from a terrible disease like cancer. Have you ever had to face anxiety and sadness and anger combined with the agony of a serious physical illness? If you've felt that way, wasn't it also hard at those times to deal with people who were healthy and optimistic and cheerful? Didn't their happy faces only serve to put a spotlight on your own misery?

For the reprobates in hell, great inner turmoil is the starting point of their day. They hurt mentally, spiritually, and physically. Their bodies reflect the depravity of their souls, and so they are deformed and diseased almost beyond recognition. Have you ever looked at yourself in the mirror and felt bad? Imagine how you'd feel if you weren't just putting on weight or getting older or losing your hair or looking more ragged but rather if you were truly grotesque and disfigured from the inside out.

Then, after this recognition of their grim reality, the very first thing the damned see when they look around is the desolation of hell. We don't know exactly what their eyes will behold, but we know it won't be appealing. We know it will consist of an absolute minimum of beauty. We know that one iota less would be nonexistence. How this lack of beauty will translate, practically speaking, is anyone's guess. Will hell be full of huge, echoing, cavernous openings in the rocks or will it be made up of small, claustrophobic coffin-like spaces deep in the bowels of the earth? Will it have barren, arid deserts and lifeless landscapes of gravel and rubble or will there perhaps be colonies of decrepit shacks or hovels or even ghostly, ruined cities? Whatever the case, hell will surely look bleak and colorless.

Now, have you ever been in surroundings you hated? In an environment that depressed you? In weather that made your spirits sink? Day after day after day? In a place filled with loud noise or rotten odors? How did it feel during those dreary moments to look on your computer or your smartphone at social media sites and see other people on vacation, splashing in pools, playing on the beach, laughing and joking with each other in sunny Caribbean climates? Maybe you were happy for them. If so, good for you. But sometimes it's hard not to feel just a little bit envious and bitter. That's the way people in hell feel when they think of the people in heaven.

And then there is the physical torment of hellfire. Hellfire—that spiritualized but very real equivalent of earthly fire—somehow lashes at their skin, burns them without consuming them, restricts their movements, and makes the very air they breathe toxic and painful. This is so hard to imagine and yet it is one of the key characteristics of hell: an environment that hurts its occupants bodily. Have you ever been in a very hot sauna or steam room for a prolonged period of time and found it difficult to breathe? Think of being trapped in such a place for hours without anything cool to drink. Think of the difficulty of trying to inhale, the discomfort involved in just moving around. That's the kind of suffocating atmosphere the reprobates have to live in all the time.

Nor do they get to suffer alone. Despite their fundamental selfishness and desire to be by themselves, they are surrounded on all sides by other creatures who despise them. First, there are the demons—pure spiritual beings who are much more powerful than humans. While suffering torments them, they are still the slave masters of hell by virtue of their greater strength. If the reprobates experience anything resembling earthly time, then certainly a good portion of their day is spent being abused by the demons, verbally as well as physically. The demons' hatred of God and humans and their own fallen condition manifests itself in this abuse much the way human beings on earth vent their anger on each other when they're upset. Indeed, the only thing close to pleasure that Satan and the demons feel is the act of sadistically imposing their will on those weaker than themselves, of causing pain to those creatures who still retain—even in this godforsaken place—the image and likeness of God.

During the course of this day, the demons inflict pain principally by putting the human reprobates through unique punishments that are actually an expression of the very sins these men and women committed in life. How exactly they do this is purely a matter of speculation. But people on earth who remain obstinate and impenitent in their pride, their faithlessness, their anger, their lust, their greed, their envy, their sloth, and their gluttony are all driven by the demons and by their own wills to act out these same desires forever in hell—only without the corresponding pleasure that accompanied the sinful behavior on earth. Thus, as noted before, the crimes themselves become the punishments.

In addition to enduring the abuse of the demons every day, the humans in hell must also endure the hideous presence of their fellow reprobates. Like the demons, some humans are more powerful in will and bodily strength and evil than others, and as a result they seek to dominate. The same slave culture that exists on earth will come to full fruition in hell, with the stronger inflicting pain on the weaker, not only to release their own hostility, but to force them to carry out their wishes. What are those wishes? Perhaps some gratification of a carnal desire, perhaps some hellish perversion (devoid of pleasure), perhaps some task or chore or form of forced labor. It's impossible to say other than that the abuser–victim dynamic will always be in play.

Possibly during the course of this day there might be some minimum amount of cooperation among the damned to achieve some common end, such as the building of a shelter or a road. But because each of the reprobates is so mired in his own ego, pride, and selfishness, any attempt at real collaboration is doomed to fail. By nightfall—if there is nighttime in hell—any cooperative efforts will have broken down. And this suits the reprobates just fine. After all, the true goal of all the humans in hell is to be alone, to get away from the demons and from each other—except insofar as interaction allows them to express their pride and their rage.

In the end, it all comes back to pride and rage.

When you hate someone with prideful passion—as those in hell hate God—everything revolves around that hatred. On earth, we see this sometimes when a person feels greatly wronged. People can become obsessed with hurting the one who wronged them. Newspapers are unfortunately filled with such examples. In the book *Moby Dick*, Captain Ahab is obsessed with his hatred for the white whale, whom he holds responsible for the loss of his leg. He doesn't care about his ship, his crew, his life. All that matters is his attempt to chase the whale and destroy him. In hell, the reprobates brood and stew and boil, just like Ahab. Their days and nights are spent thinking about the wrongs they have endured and about their own massive, wounded pride. They play the recordings of these grievances over and over in their minds, whipping themselves into an even greater frenzy, with the end result always the same anguished cry: "I don't care how much I have to suffer, I hate God. I hate all that he is and all that he does. I hate all the happy, cursed people in heaven. I hate the angels. I hate the demons. I hate these other disgusting human beings. I hate my life. I want to do what *I* want to do. I'll roast here forever before I go crawling back to that evil monster who made me and ruined me. I don't care about the pain. I don't care about hell! I don't care about anything—except *me!*"

And so it goes. Day after day. Year after year. Always the same despair. Always the same resentment. Always the same lashing out in anger. A lifetime of hellish Mondays. A lifetime fixed in fury.

fourteen

Hell on Earth

Front-Row Seats to Immortal Combat

U p to this point, we've only talked about hell as a future reality, as a place where rebellious, unfaithful, and impenitent sinners go after they die. But that's not the whole story. Hell can be part of the present as well. It's actually similar to heaven in that way.

In the Gospels, Christ said, "The kingdom of heaven is at hand."[1] He meant that by entrusting ourselves to him with the "obedience of faith,"[2] we can get a taste of heaven right now. Scripture tells us that Christ is actually *in* us, that he is our "hope of glory,"[3] and that he enables us to walk in the path of all his commandments. Thus, grace is not only invisible help from God, but it is also an inner condition or quality of the soul that represents the beginning of everlasting life. You might say it represents the seed of our lives in heaven beginning to blossom during our lives on earth. A person who lives in union with God can experience many of the joys of heaven in the present moment, no matter what his situation, and even if he is suffering terribly. As the apostle Paul said, God has the power to give us a peace that "transcends all understanding."[4]

But unfortunately, in addition to a kingdom of heaven, there is also a kingdom of hell, and it also represents an inner condition of the soul and a way of living that can give us a foretaste of the future—the future of the damned.

Earlier we talked about Satan and his cohort of fallen angels and how these demons continue to rebel against God today. Basically, they have two ways of doing this. One is to try to make the life of human beings a hell on earth. The other is to induce as many human beings as possible to go to hell after they die.[5]

Why in the world would they want to do that?

It all goes back to their hatred of God. The demons want to offend their creator. They want to hurt him. They want to taunt him. But they can't do that directly, because God is almighty, or as the theologians say, he is impassible, which means he is incapable of being harmed.[6] Therefore, the demons do what *is* possible for them—they try to hurt God's children.

If you're a parent, then you certainly understand this reasoning. What's the worst thing anyone could ever do to you? Isn't it to go after your children? Isn't it to hurt them? Isn't it to threaten them? Well, *we* are God's children. We're made in his image and likeness. And while God can't be hurt in his divine nature, he also has a human nature. Christians believe that Jesus Christ is fully God *and* fully man. In his human nature, God is actually capable of feeling sorrow. He is capable of being hurt. When Jesus walked on the earth two thousand years ago, he wept when his friend Lazarus died. Today, that same Jesus who wept for Lazarus lives in heaven and is able to weep for us. This is one of the great paradoxes of Christianity. God is all-powerful, but in some mysterious way he can still experience suffering. And he suffers most when his children are attacked. So if the devil really wants to lash out at God, he attacks human beings.

How does he do that?

One very well-known way is through the phenomenon of demonic possession. Catholics and Protestants alike believe in the malevolence and power of the demons. The New Testament couldn't be clearer on this score. The devil is a very real threat, as the apostle Peter warned: "Be alert and of sober mind. Your enemy the devil prowls around like a roaring lion looking for someone to devour."[7] In the Gospels, we see that genuine cases of possession were frequently encountered by Jesus and his apostles.[8] Likewise, Paul performed several exorcisms during his ministry.[9] The history of the early church is filled with instances of similar diabolical agency. To deny this would be to rewrite Scripture.

Well, the devil continues today to have the power to assume control of a person's body from within. As we know from the teaching of the church fathers and other Christian theologians, the soul itself can never be possessed or deprived of liberty, but the actions of the physical body may indeed be influenced by demonic spirits, especially if consent is given by the person in terms of their indulgence in diabolical evil.

Nowadays, this is very rare. Most reported cases of possession are not real but simply due to mental or emotional problems. However, the recognition of the existence of psychological abnormalities is not the only reason there are fewer instances of demonic possession. Another factor is simply that the devil's game plan has changed over time. So many people today have lost faith in God. They've become skeptical and agnostic and atheistic, and that's a very good, easy way for the devil to lead them off the path to heaven. Nor does the devil have to possess people's bodies in order to cause them suffering. In fact, why bother possessing people in such secular times as these when the main result would probably be to increase the general belief that God exists? After all, if you're an agnostic, wouldn't seeing an actual case of demonic possession—complete with plates flying and furniture moving and someone throwing up green slime—cause you to believe in the invisible spiritual world? Wouldn't it cause you to believe more in the devil and consequently in God? From the devil's point of view, the best way to lead a person to hell is to stifle their faith, not strengthen it with overt displays of supernatural power. As someone observed long ago, the goal of the devil is to make people believe he *doesn't* exist, to remain completely hidden and anonymous. If God's chosen name is I am, the devil's is I am not.

Therefore, possessing a human being—even when the human being in question invites that possession—is actually quite counterproductive to the aims of the devil and his demons.

Far better and more effective than possession is the attempt by the devil to *tempt* people to believe certain things and act in certain sinful ways. This is what Paul was primarily talking about when he said: "Our wrestling is not against flesh and blood; but against principalities and powers, against the rulers of the world of this darkness, against the spirits of wickedness in the high places."[10]

As I discussed more fully in my book *Inside the Atheist Mind*, from the moment the serpent tempted our first parents in the garden of Eden, dark spiritual forces have tried to trick, deceive, injure, humiliate, mock, and murder human beings. Their strategy has always been the same: to use deception to convince them to abuse their freedom and make them think they can have all the power they want if only they disregard the will of God. The point of the story of the fall of man is not that Adam and Eve ate a piece of fruit that was forbidden to them, but that human beings, at the instigation of the devil, freely chose to turn away from God in prideful disobedience to *make themselves into gods*. And as a result of that selfish decision, sin, suffering, and death entered the world.[11]

What's so frightening about the tragedy of the fall of man is that the same diabolical dynamic exists today. It actually hasn't changed one bit. Consider the following satanic strategy.

At the center of Christianity is the concept of repentance. Repentance simply means being sorry for sin, and being sorry for sin entails turning away from evil and back to God. Repentance thus represents a reversal of the sin of pride, a reversal of the original sin that was committed by the devil and his demons and by our first parents in Eden. It is an undoing of our rebellious nature and a sign of true faith. Christians believe that this turning back to God in faith is an absolute prerequisite to entering heaven and achieving full union with God.[12]

Christians also believe that God has made repentance very easy for us. In fact, if you turn away from God by sinning, all you have to do is say you're sorry and God will forgive you, no matter what the sin and no matter how many times you've committed it. We don't have time to go into the theology of redemption, but the bottom line is that because of Christ's sacrifice on the cross, God has set the bar very low when it comes to forgiving our sins. Indeed, he has already done all the heavy work of redemption for us.[13] All we have to do is ask for forgiveness with sincerity and he will grant it.* The heart of the Christian gospel is mercy.

The problem is this: the devil understands the concept of forgiveness too. He isn't stupid. He can read the Bible as well as we can. So when he goes about the business of temptation, he's extremely aware that the person he's trying to lead away from God may thwart all his plans with a simple last-minute apology. Therefore, his strategy turns on something else, that is, on an effort to ensure that the person he's tempting *doesn't repent in the first place*.

When you get right down to it, the devil doesn't have a complicated plan for winning souls. In fact, it's very simple. There are basically three kinds of beliefs or attitudes he and his demons try to get every human being to adopt. Let's take them one at a time.

First, there is atheism, which destroys the very possibility of repentance. The reason is obvious. If you don't believe in God, there isn't anyone for you to apologize to. Why say you're sorry for committing a sin when no one is even listening?

If that doesn't work, there's a second tactic the devil can use that's just as effective. If he can't get you to disbelieve in God, he can try to make you disbelieve in God's mercy. This way of thinking and feeling is known as despair, and the way the devil tries to instill despair is by whispering such things as "There may be a God, but your sins are so terrible, he would never forgive

---

* Different traditions have different ways of expressing repentance. For example, the Catholic church has an added sacrament of reconciliation.

you. You might as well just keep doing what you're doing, because you're lost anyway." This is an extraordinarily effective method of destroying souls and one that's very easy for the devil to employ, since so many of us fall into the same sins over and over again. It's simple for him to inject the idea into our heads that there's no hope, that it's pointless even to approach God, because he's so disgusted or angry with us.

If both these methods fail, there's one other highly effective thing that can be tried: the devil can attempt to make you into a moral relativist. This is the ethical system that says that there's no such thing as objective truth. Human beings are free to make their own rules and dispense with all biblical commandments. The devil tries to get us to adopt this kind of thinking by saying things like: "Don't be a fool! *You* determine what's right and what's wrong. All of morality is relative. You're the only one who can decide what's true for you, and you can't let any book or any church or any god determine what's best for your life."

This is, of course, the same lie spoken by the serpent in the garden of Eden, the same philosophy that seduced Adam and Eve. It's Nietzsche's superman idea all over again, and it is an extremely potent antidote against repentance. When human beings adopt moral relativism, there's no need for them to repent of their sins, because they don't think they've committed any sins. They don't believe sin exists, so why apologize if there is nothing to be sorry for? Once more, the devil's diabolical objective has been achieved.

You see, it's very important to understand the brilliance of the Enemy with whom we're contending. Remember, the two main words used for him in Scripture—Satan and the devil— mean the adversary or the accuser or the one who scatters. The

Bible also calls him "a liar," "the father of lies," and "a murderer from the beginning."[14] These aren't empty words and phrases. They represent the deepest truth about the evil one. They represent qualities that are diametrically opposed to who God is. Our God is a God of abundant life, a God of truth, a God who gathers his people together in a family, because he *is* a family within himself—Father, Son and Holy Spirit.[15] The devil hurts God most effectively by tempting humans to do things completely contrary to all these divine attributes. Thus, whenever we see untruthfulness or finger-pointing or malicious gossip or fighting in families or assaults on the idea of the family itself or any kind of attack on innocent human life, the devil is usually at work.

And looking at the world we live in today, it's hard to argue that the devil hasn't done an excellent job. Not only do we see masses of people choosing to turn away from faith in God and from the very concept of repentance, but we also see the effects of those choices manifested all over the world. We are entrenched in a culture of atheistic deceit, despair, relativism, and death. And the result has been just what we said it would be at the beginning of this chapter. We've been given a foretaste of hell.

Just look at the facts. Crime rates have skyrocketed. Murders, rapes, and incidents of child molestation are at all-time highs. Likewise, addiction to alcohol, drugs, and pornography are on the rise. The global divorce rate is now 44 percent, which has increased 251.8 percent since 1960. The number of suicides is shocking—more than a million a year, with someone taking his or her own life every forty seconds. Worldwide abortions are up to fifteen million a year—a billion since the early 1960s. The use of euthanasia and assisted suicide to prematurely kill adults and children—with or without terminal diseases—is becoming routine across the globe.[16] As a society we are up to our necks in innocent blood.

Of course, the culture of death and despair is more than just statistics. As we've discussed, it's about being held captive to sin. Human beings lose their freedom by abusing their freedom. In forfeiting God's laws and adopting the rebellious attitude of the devil, we've consequently become a race of slaves.

And with that slavery has come a host of other afflictions, all of them straight out of hell: stress, fear, desolation, emptiness, loneliness, and hopelessness. In the twenty-first century we are not a happy people, despite our economic prosperity and technological advances. On the contrary, we are a world mired in misery and anxiety.

Maybe you've experienced some of this in your own life. Be honest with yourself. When you've left the straight path for any length of time and knowingly indulged in sins of whatever kind, what has been the result? Isn't it true that things have tended to fall apart around you, including your relationships? Hasn't chaos crept into your life? Haven't you felt overwhelmed by events you might otherwise have handled easily? There's a reason for this. The very nature of sin is disorder and disintegration. That's because sin represents a severing of ties with God, who *is* order.[17] So if you persist in rebelling against order, it's inevitable that turmoil will result.

Now, the most common effect of this breakdown in order is *fear*. When you're not doing well morally, and you know it but keep sinning anyway, you begin to experience a deep-seated dread about life in general. Remember this theological truth: the devil is a master terrorist. His object is to frighten you. Moreover, he is a ruthless enemy and an opportunist who always attacks you at your weakest point, whether that's mentally, emotionally, psychologically, spiritually, or a combination of all four. The devil will attempt to cultivate in your soul a fear for your family, a fear for your finances, a fear for your health, a fear for everything that's important to you. Most of all, he will try to convince you that you don't have the ability to deal with your problems, that you don't have what it takes to overcome the obstacles you face—not even with the help of grace.

The diabolical cycle of temptation goes like this:

1. The devil uses lies to encourage you to rebel against God in the form of sin.
2. He then uses your repeated sins to make you a slave to sin.
3. After he has enslaved you for a period of time, he does his best to convince you that you are powerless to conquer your sins, as well as any of the other challenges in your life.
4. This leads to hopelessness, which leads to even more sinning (after all, why bother to resist?) and even more fear, disorder, and despair.

This is the vicious strategy the devil and his demons continually employ on human beings of every age and in every segment of society. And it is a dim intimation of what life in hell will be like: a life of fear, compulsion, hopelessness, desolation, misery, and slavery.

The overarching goal of the devil is to keep this cycle going for as long as he can, right up until you die. The instant of your death is really what he is most concerned about. Yes, he loves

causing you pain and inciting you to sin against God throughout your life, but the moment of death is really the moment of
truth—both for him and for you. It's the last pitch to the last
batter in the last inning. It's the final play of the fourth quarter.
It's the closing of the curtain in the play's last act. It's the very
end of the fighting at the conclusion of the war. Will all the time
and effort the devil spent working to cultivate evil in your soul
go up in smoke with a deathbed, faith-filled conversion or will it
pay infernal dividends throughout eternity?

If you could only imagine the battle that rages around a
human being shortly before death! If you could only see the
spiritual warfare taking place! Christianity teaches that it is a
time of incredible, invisible activity. Immortal combat is taking
place between the devil and his demons on one side, God's grace
on the other, and the totally free will of a human being in the
middle. Every time someone dies, no matter what the circumstances, no matter if it's the result of a long illness or a sudden
tragedy, the soul of one of God's children hangs in the balance,
and there is a furious campaign on both sides to win it.

Remember this when you feel yourself in danger of becoming captive to sin. If the devil can get you to keep on rebelling
without repenting, to keep on despairing without hoping, to keep
on disbelieving without trusting—right up till the end—then
your final choice against God will be fixed forever the second
your soul leaves your body. You will have made your decision to
be permanently enslaved in prideful impenitence. And then, no
matter what good you've done before, the forces of darkness will
have you. Game. Set. Match.

But wait! The curtain hasn't descended quite yet. At the
end of *A Christmas Carol*, Ebenezer Scrooge asks the Ghost of

Christmas Yet to Come if the scenes he has been shown are the shadows of things that *will* be or *might* be. When it comes to the subject of hell, the answer to that question—for those of us who are still alive—is always the latter. As long as there's life, there's hope. Before we end this tour, we need to focus all our attention on this supremely important point.

Ticket to Hell?

Deciding Whether or Not to Make the Trip

Yes, if you're reading these words, there's still time left. God desires no one to go to hell.[1] There is absolutely no sin in the world that can't be forgiven, except final impenitence, that is, the sin of not wanting to be forgiven. That is the unpardonable sin against the Holy Spirit that Christ spoke about in the Gospels.[2] And it is unpardonable not because of God but because of man. The Holy Spirit is the spirit of mercy. If you turn away from that mercy, then there's nothing anyone can do about it, not even God almighty.

It's just nonsense when people think they're too sinful to be forgiven. That kind of scrupulosity is nothing but pride. Do these great sinners really think their sins are greater than God's mercy?

Greater than his grace? Greater than his power? If you believe that, then you'd better wake up and stop being so arrogant! As I've said and as spiritual writers much better than I have said down through the centuries, one drop of Christ's blood is enough to wash away the sins of a billion universes.

Listen, you're always going to experience setbacks and falls and lapses in the spiritual life. You're always going to have to contend with pride and carnality and the other deadly sins. You're always going to have to deal with habitual or compulsive problems and the many things in life that trigger such behavior. But no matter what you do, as long as you sincerely desire to turn back to God, you can be forgiven. As the Bible says, "Though your sins are like scarlet, they shall be as white as snow."[3] And as the great Fulton Sheen said, it doesn't matter what sin you've committed or how many times you've committed it, you're not the worst person in the world; the worst person in the world is the one who thinks he's the best person.[4] As long as you're humble enough to know you have fallen short of the mark and need forgiving, then you're not going to hell. Period. Ultimately the definition of a spiritually successful life is one in which you faithfully repent one more time than you sin, one in which you faithfully get back up one more time than you fall.

So as we come to the end of this book on the horrors of hell, remember never to despair. In this war against hell, we are assured victory *as long as we are willing to fight*. Indeed, God has set the bar extremely low when it comes to getting into heaven. As we've said, his Son, Jesus Christ, has already accomplished the hard work of redemption for us. In dying on the cross and rising from the dead, he has given us the antidote to everlasting death. All we have to do is take it. And one of the primary ways of taking that antidote is to make sure we're sorry whenever we sin.

At the same time, while you need to understand that God's very name is mercy, you can't for a moment listen to the skeptics who say there is no such thing as hell or that people don't go there. That would be a huge and potentially deadly mistake. Hell, like heaven, is real.

Read through the appendix at the end of this book that lists all the Bible verses that speak so forcefully about hell, the devil, and the demons. Read it slowly and carefully and honestly, as a person of faith. After you finish, ask yourself these questions: Do you really think all these quotes are *symbolic* in substance? Do you really think that none of them correspond to the literal truth?

What arrogance it is to believe that, to believe that God has misspoken or even lied on so many different occasions. God doesn't lie. And on a matter as serious as this, he certainly wouldn't accidentally mislead us.[5]

In fact, not only do the words of Christ and the clear teaching of his church for two thousand years testify to the real existence of hell, but so does common sense. So does reason itself.

Follow me here! What would be the point of all the suffering and sorrow we have to go through in life if there was nothing important at stake? If, at the end of the world, God simply said, "Okay, all of you can come into paradise, even those who hate me, who reject me, who are so prideful they won't even admit their sins. All of you come in and let's have a big party. The slate is wiped clean."

If that were the case, why should Christ have suffered such an agonizing death on the cross? Why should he have even bothered to go through the humiliation of the incarnation and the passion? Christianity has always taught that one of the main reasons God became a man and endured such pain and anguish is because the consequences of sin require it. His death shows in no uncertain terms that "the wages of sin is death."[6] We need to truly grasp how serious it is to rebel against God. So serious, in fact, that it necessitated the bloody sacrifice of his only Son to redeem us.

Whenever we rebel against God, whenever we go through some kind of terrible fear or grief or trial, we can always look at the cross and say, "God hates sin and death so much that he went through *that* in order to save us. He went through *that* in order to give us everlasting life, just as long as we choose to have faith in him and turn back to him when we fall and imitate him as best we can."

But if God just hands out free passes to heaven—despite any lack of faith or repentance or humility on our part—then why did he bother going through the agony of that awful crucifixion? Why make us go through the obscenity of suffering and death? How serious can it be to rebel against God if he intended all along to permit us be as evil as we like, if he intended all along to give us a cosmic Get Out of Jail Free card?

This point is critical to understand. If you take away sin and hell and the devil—as secularists and many liberal theologians in the church want to do—then you do three things. First, you strip humans of free will. Second, you make a mockery of God's will. Third, you deprive life on this planet of any real meaning. After all, what's the point of a test if there's no possibility of failing? What's the point of a game if there's no possibility of losing? What's the point of an adventure if there's no possibility of incurring risk?

Paul said to the Jews who didn't believe in the resurrection, "If the dead are not raised, 'Let us eat and drink, for tomorrow we die.'"[7] Well, the same thing can be said to Christians today who deny hell and believe instead in universalism or annihilationism. "If there's no chance of going to hell, then let's sin as much as we want. Let's eat, drink, be merry, cheat on our spouses, steal as much as we can, rape whoever we want, murder whoever gets in our way, indulge every nasty or perverted thought that comes into our heads, and then, when we're done, thumb our noses at God, reject his gospel, and curse him too! Just do whatever we want! After all, it won't make any difference, because we're all going to heaven anyway!"

Again, if there's no real choice between heaven and hell, then why would God put us through the hell involved in living in this crazy world? If you do away with hell, then you ultimately trivialize life. Nothing justifies human suffering unless there is something to suffer *for*. The fact that suffering purifies us, prepares us, tests us, strengthens us, and makes us more Christlike is meaningful only to the extent that there is really something to be won—and something to be lost. If you take away the possibility of hell, you take away the whole value of suffering. And if you take away the value of suffering, you take away the meaning of love and honor and pity. You make all the sacrifices of life a preposterous joke. If God just waves a magic wand at the end of time and makes everyone happy forever—or if he turns evil souls into a puff of smoke—then the game truly has been rigged from the beginning. Evil really has no consequences, and there really is no such thing as justice or free will.

The bottom line is this: if you're not free to choose evil—with all its terrible ramifications—then you're not truly free.

And you *know* very well you're free. You know at every moment of your life you have the ability to make some very bad, very evil decisions. The whole point of Christianity is that we get to choose our fate, that we get to choose for or against God. Today, those lines are easier to see than ever before. Just take a look at the spiritual war raging around us. Every one of the commandments is under attack. Christian morality is under attack. The family is under attack. The church is under attack. Religious freedom is under attack. Free speech is under attack. The unborn are under attack. The old and the infirm are under attack. The very underpinnings of society are under attack. You have to be blind not to see what's happening! We are immersed in an epic spiritual conflict between life and death, truth and lies, humility and pride, light and darkness, good and evil.

And we are privileged to have a role in this spiritual battle. We are privileged to be able to choose sides, to decide whether to tolerate and embrace evil or to fight against it with all our might. Remember, Christ left us with a very clear command: make disciples of all nations, struggle against injustice no matter what persecution and pain we must endure. In fact, the joy we experience as Christians becomes more real and intense when we actively take up the fight against evil in a courageous way instead of just trying to live a comfortable Christianity. That's the decision we all have before us: fight evil or cowardly acquiesce to it. In fact, that decision—next to our decision to have faith in Christ—is the single most important choice we'll ever make in life.[8]

But all of it means nothing if there is no such thing as hell!

Once and for all, it's the existence of hell that makes our decision about evil *matter*. It's what gives it all its meaning and gravity. Without hell, the war between good and evil wouldn't be a war at all. In fact, it wouldn't even be a skirmish. Who cares about the attacks on the family and the attacks on the church and the attacks on our values and the attacks on life if there's no ultimate justice and no ultimate consequences?

Which brings us back to a question we raised at the very start of this book. Even if we accept the existence of hell as a doctrine of faith, why read a travel guide to such a place? Why not just have a pleasant, rational discussion about the nature of good and evil? Or about the nature of free will? Or even about the idea of hell in the abstract? Why bother to flesh out all the gory details of Gehenna? Why subject ourselves to such a horrid, masochistic display of suffering, when life itself is already so full of pain?

The simple reason is we can't make any lasting decision to fight against our own evil inclinations and against the evil times in which we live unless we know what lies at the bottom of the struggle, unless we know what the root cause of the combat really is. In other words, we can't make any monumental choice *for* or *against* God unless we have access to all the facts. And hell, though tremendously disagreeable, is a *fact*.

Moreover, it's a fact that must be addressed not only as an abstract spiritual concept but as a concrete, physical reality. To really understand the depths of diabolical darkness, we have to get down into the muck. Like Dante in his *Inferno*, we have to abase ourselves and search the inmost core of our beings and our own capacity for evil. We have to identify the Satan who lives and hides in our bowels, beating the icy cold, evil air at the bottom of our souls with his wings, driving that evil wind into our minds and thoughts and words and deeds in order to create a toxic atmosphere of hell in our lives. We have to understand that very real demonic dynamic—both psychologically and metaphysically—before we can make a true ascent, with faith and courage, out of hell and into a new daylight of our souls.

Human reason alone isn't enough for this journey of discovery. True humility is necessary. As we said at the beginning of this guide, we have to go down before we can go up. We have to pass through the darkness and even be immersed in it in order to finally see the light. Essentially we have to recognize and repent of evil before we can be forgiven. We have to be crucified before we can experience resurrection.[9]

Visualizing the torments of hell is the best way to do this because it involves mortifying our pride. It involves accepting the fact that we are nothing without God. It doesn't matter how smart or pretty or rich or powerful we happen to be. Without God, we are doomed to unhappiness. Without God, there is no truth, no goodness, no beauty, no grace, no growth, no love, no joy. Without God, there is only one thing—hell.

That's why this trip has been necessary.

Of course, there's a whole lot more to the spiritual life than trying to avoid hell. That's only the beginning. Thomas Aquinas said, "If the highest aim of a captain were to preserve his ship, he would keep it in port forever." But it's not the highest aim. The purpose of having a ship is to journey to some far-off destination, to go on an adventure, to experience joy. Likewise, the main objective in life is not only to repent of sin but to *stop* sinning. Not just to stop sinning, but to advance in holiness.

We've talked a lot in this book about the devil and how much he wants to destroy human beings. That's absolutely true. But it's also true that you can't be afraid of him, especially if you're a committed Christian. Someone once said that the devil is like a vicious dog on a six-foot chain. The most effective counterstrategy to all his terrible attacks and temptations can be summed up in five little words: *don't get in his range!*

If you want to avoid being trapped in the jaws of the evil one, you can't get too close to evil. It's that simple. And the best way to avoid evil is to stop sinning grievously.[10] Sinning—and in particular obstinate sinning—is the equivalent of running away from God and into the devil's arms. If you stay far enough away from the devil, all he can do is bark and try to frighten you. He's just another harmless dog on a chain. The only way he can hurt you is if you give yourself to him.

So don't!

Now, once you've gotten some measure of self-control and self-discipline, you can start doing even more in the spiritual life. You can try to grow in faith and love and strive to be in an ever-closer union with God. Indeed, the deepest purpose of life is to know, love, and serve God—and then to be happy with him forever in paradise.

How exactly can you accomplish that? Different traditions in Christianity emphasize different routes to reach the Almighty: faith, baptism, prayer, fasting, penance, virtue, the sacraments. But all the traditions agree on one thing: *you must go through Jesus Christ.* Whether you know it or not, accept it or not, believe it or not—he is the Lord. He is the victor over sin and death. He is the gate to eternal happiness. He is "the way and the truth and the life."[11]

Christ is the means to enlarging your soul. Ultimately, that's what the spiritual life is all about—enlarging your soul to such a degree that it can hold the maximum amount of God, trying to adopt an attitude of total childlike trust, openness, and wonder in order to radiate the joy of Christ in all your actions, no matter what your circumstances, no matter what your suffering. The more in union you are with God, the more truth and goodness and beauty and joy you will feel right here on earth and then, later on, in heaven.

Yes, heaven!

> Eye has not seen, nor ear heard,
> Nor have entered into the heart of man
> The things which God has prepared for those who
> love Him.[12]

What a different kind of place heaven is than hell. And what a different kind of travel guide to describe it! Instead of being dark and frightening, heaven will be lit up with bright light from a sun that never sets and bursting with more dazzling colors than any we've ever known. Instead of being a barren, malignant wasteland, it will be filled with every conceivable form of life in a spectacular setting to match it, with magnificent mountains and valleys and rivers and oceans and forests. Instead of being a place of drudgery and slavery, it will be a land of activity and energy and music and learning and freedom and fun. Instead of being a gloomy prison of lost souls, with all its hopeless, tragic inmates at war with one another, it will be a glorious city whose citizens share the deepest possible bonds of affection and intimacy and love.[13]

And if you are blessed to go to this wondrous place someday after you die and see your loved ones again, you won't just be seeing wispy, invisible spirits. After the resurrection, your friends and family will be real, living human beings with glorified bodies and warm, vibrant flesh and clear, recognizable voices. And you'll be able to embrace them and spend time with them and reminisce with them and laugh with them and go on new adventures with them and enjoy life for all eternity with them.

But that sightseeing trip to heaven, God's ultimate playground, is a different tour for a different day. The present tour—thank goodness—is ended.

*   *   *

My guide and I came to a hidden road and made our way back into the bright world. With no desire to rest, we climbed—he first, I following—until I saw, through a round opening, some of the beauty of the sky. It was from there that we emerged to behold—once more—the stars.

—The final lines of Dante's **Inferno** (author's translation)

Acknowledgments

I would like to express my gratitude to all the good people at Thomas Nelson, especially my brilliant editors, Brigitta Nortker and Webster Younce. I would also like to thank my literary manager, Peter Miller, my gifted research assistant, Jonathan Caulk, and finally, my beautiful wife, Jordan.

Appendix

Hell, Satan, and the Demons in the Bible

Hell

Deuteronomy 30:19: This day I call the heavens and the earth as witnesses against you that I have set before you life and death, blessings and curses. Now choose life, so that you and your children may live.

Isaiah 66:23–24: "All mankind will come and bow down before me," says the LORD. "And they will go out and look on the dead bodies of those who rebelled against me; the worms that eat them will not die, the fire that burns them will not be quenched, and they will be loathsome to all mankind."

Jeremiah 21:8: Furthermore, tell the people, "This is what the LORD says: See, I am setting before you the way of life and the way of death."

Daniel 12:2: Multitudes who sleep in the dust of the earth will awake: some to everlasting life, others to shame and everlasting contempt.

Matthew 3:7, 12: But when he saw many of the Pharisees and Sadducees coming to where he was baptizing, he said to them: "You brood of vipers! Who warned you to flee from the coming wrath? . . . His winnowing fork is in his hand, and he will clear his threshing floor, gathering his wheat into the barn and burning up the chaff with unquenchable fire."

Matthew 5:22: But I tell you that anyone who is angry with a brother or sister will be subject to judgment. Again, anyone who says to a brother or sister, "Raca," is answerable to the court. And anyone who says, "You fool!" will be in danger of the fire of hell.

Matthew 5:29–30: If your right eye causes you to stumble, gouge it out and throw it away. It is better for you to lose one part of your body than for your whole body to be thrown into hell. And if your right hand causes you to stumble, cut it off and throw it away. It is better for you to lose one part of your body than for your whole body to go into hell.

Matthew 7:13: Enter through the narrow gate. For wide is the gate and broad is the road that leads to destruction, and many enter through it.

Matthew 8:12: But the subjects of the kingdom will be thrown outside, into the darkness, where there will be weeping and gnashing of teeth.

Matthew 10:28: Do not be afraid of those who kill the body but cannot kill the soul. Rather, be afraid of the One who can destroy both soul and body in hell.

Matthew 13:38–42: The field is the world, and the good seed stands for the people of the kingdom. The weeds are the people of the evil one, and the enemy who sows them is the devil. The harvest is the end of the age, and the harvesters are angels.

As the weeds are pulled up and burned in the fire, so it will be at the end of the age. The Son of Man will send out his angels, and they will weed out of his kingdom everything that causes sin and all who do evil. They will throw them into the blazing furnace, where there will be weeping and gnashing of teeth.

Matthew 13:49–50: This is how it will be at the end of the age. The angels will come and separate the wicked from the righteous and throw them into the blazing furnace, where there will be weeping and gnashing of teeth.

Matthew 16:18 (KJV): And I say also unto thee, That thou art Peter, and upon this rock I will build my church; and the gates of hell shall not prevail against it.

Matthew 18:8–9: If your hand or your foot causes you to stumble, cut it off and throw it away. It is better for you to enter life maimed or crippled than to have two hands or two feet and be thrown into eternal fire. And if your eye causes you to stumble, gouge it out and throw it away. It is better for you to enter life with one eye than to have two eyes and be thrown into the fire of hell.

Matthew 23:15: Woe to you, teachers of the law and Pharisees, you hypocrites! You travel over land and sea to win a single convert, and when you have succeeded, you make them twice as much a child of hell as you are.

Matthew 23:33: You snakes! You brood of vipers! How will you escape being condemned to hell?

Matthew 25:30: And throw that worthless servant outside, into the darkness, where there will be weeping and gnashing of teeth.

Matthew 25:41: Then he will say to those on his left, "Depart from me, you who are cursed, into the eternal fire prepared for the devil and his angels."

Matthew 25:46: Then they will go away to eternal punishment, but the righteous to eternal life.

Mark 3:29: But whoever blasphemes against the Holy Spirit will never be forgiven; they are guilty of an eternal sin.

Mark 9:43–49: If your hand causes you to stumble, cut it off. It is better for you to enter life maimed than with two hands to go into hell, where the fire never goes out. And if your foot causes you to stumble, cut it off. It is better for you to enter life crippled than to have two feet and be thrown into hell. And if your eye causes you to stumble, pluck it out. It is better for you to enter the kingdom of God with one eye than to have two eyes and be thrown into hell, where "the worms that eat them do not die, and the fire is not quenched."
Everyone will be salted with fire.

Luke 12:5: But I will show you whom you should fear: Fear him who, after your body has been killed, has authority to throw you into hell. Yes, I tell you, fear him.

Luke 13:27–28: But he will reply, "I don't know you or where you come from. Away from me, all you evildoers!"
There will be weeping there, and gnashing of teeth, when you see Abraham, Isaac and Jacob and all the prophets in the kingdom of God, but you yourselves thrown out.

John 3:36: Whoever believes in the Son has eternal life, but whoever rejects the Son will not see life, for God's wrath remains on them.

Romans 2:5: But because of your stubbornness and your unrepentant heart, you are storing up wrath against yourself for the day of God's wrath, when his righteous judgment will be revealed.

Philippians 3:18–19: For, as I have often told you before and now tell you again even with tears, many live as enemies of the cross of Christ. Their destiny is destruction, their god is their stomach, and their glory is in their shame. Their mind is set on earthly things.

2 Thessalonians 1:8–9: He will punish those who do not know God and do not obey the gospel of our Lord Jesus. They will be punished with everlasting destruction and shut out from the presence of the Lord and from the glory of his might.

Hebrews 6:1–2: Therefore let us move beyond the elementary teachings about Christ and be taken forward to maturity, not laying again the foundation of repentance from acts that lead to death, and of faith in God, instruction about cleansing rites, the laying on of hands, the resurrection of the dead, and eternal judgment.

Hebrews 10:26–27: If we deliberately keep on sinning after we have received the knowledge of the truth, no sacrifice for sins is left, but only a fearful expectation of judgment and of raging fire that will consume the enemies of God.

James 3:6: The tongue also is a fire, a world of evil among the parts of the body. It corrupts the whole body, sets the whole course of one's life on fire, and is itself set on fire by hell.

2 Peter 2:4: For if God did not spare angels when they sinned, but sent them to hell, putting them in chains of darkness to be held for judgment . . .

Jude 6–7, 13: And the angels who did not keep their positions of authority but abandoned their proper dwelling—these he has kept in darkness, bound with everlasting chains for judgment on the great Day. In a similar way, Sodom and Gomorrah and the surrounding towns gave themselves up to sexual immorality and perversion. They serve as an example of those who suffer the punishment of eternal fire. . . .

. . . They are wild waves of the sea, foaming up their shame; wandering stars, for whom blackest darkness has been reserved forever.

Revelation 9:2: When he opened the Abyss, smoke rose from it like the smoke from a gigantic furnace. The sun and sky were darkened by the smoke from the Abyss.

Revelation 9:11: They had as king over them the angel of the Abyss, whose name in Hebrew is Abaddon and in Greek is Apollyon (that is, Destroyer).

Revelation 14:10–11: They, too, will drink the wine of God's fury, which has been poured full strength into the cup of his wrath. They will be tormented with burning sulfur in the presence of the holy angels and of the Lamb. And the smoke of their torment will rise for ever and ever. There will be no rest day or night for those who worship the beast and its image, or for anyone who receives the mark of its name.

Revelation 19:20: But the beast was captured, and with it the false prophet who had performed the signs on its behalf. With these signs he had deluded those who had received the mark of the beast and worshiped its image. The two of them were thrown alive into the fiery lake of burning sulfur.

Revelation 20:10: And the devil, who deceived them, was thrown into the lake of burning sulfur, where the beast and the false prophet had been thrown. They will be tormented day and night for ever and ever.

Revelation 20:13: The sea gave up the dead that were in it, and death and Hades gave up the dead that were in them, and each person was judged according to what they had done.

Revelation 20:14–15: Then death and Hades were thrown into the lake of fire. The lake of fire is the second death. Anyone whose name was not found written in the book of life was thrown into the lake of fire.

Revelation 21:8: But the cowardly, the unbelieving, the vile, the murderers, the sexually immoral, those who practice magic arts, the idolaters and all liars—they will be consigned to the fiery lake of burning sulfur.

Satan and the Demons

Isaiah 14:12–15: How you have fallen from heaven,
morning star, son of the dawn!
You have been cast down to the earth,
you who once laid low the nations!
You said in your heart,
"I will ascend to the heavens;
I will raise my throne
above the stars of God; . . .
I will ascend above the tops of the clouds;
I will make myself like the Most High."
But you are brought down to the realm of the dead,
to the depths of the pit.

1 Chronicles 21:1: Satan rose up against Israel and incited David to take a census of Israel.

Job 1:6–8: One day the angels came to present themselves before the Lord, and Satan also came with them. The Lord said to Satan, "Where have you come from?"

Satan answered the Lord, "From roaming throughout the earth, going back and forth on it."

Then the Lord said to Satan, "Have you considered my servant Job? There is no one on earth like him;

he is blameless and upright, a man who fears God and shuns evil."

Zechariah 3:1–2: Then he showed me Joshua the high priest standing before the angel of the LORD, and Satan standing at his right side to accuse him. The LORD said to Satan, "The LORD rebuke you, Satan! The LORD, who has chosen Jerusalem, rebuke you! Is not this man a burning stick snatched from the fire?"

Matthew 4:1: Then Jesus was led by the Spirit into the wilderness to be tempted by the devil.

Matthew 4:5–11: Then the devil took him to the holy city and had him stand on the highest point of the temple. "If you are the Son of God," he said, "throw yourself down. For it is written:

"'He will command his angels concerning you,
and they will lift you up in their hands,
so that you will not strike your foot against a stone.'"

Jesus answered him, "It is also written: 'Do not put the Lord your God to the test.'"

Again, the devil took him to a very high mountain and showed him all the kingdoms of the world and their splendor. "All this I will give you," he said, "if you will bow down and worship me."

Jesus said to him, "Away from me, Satan! For it is

written: 'Worship the Lord your God, and serve him only.'"

Then the devil left him, and angels came and attended him.

Matthew 12:24: But when the Pharisees heard this, they said, "It is only by Beelzebub, the prince of demons, that this fellow drives out demons."

Matthew 12:26: If Satan drives out Satan, he is divided against himself. How then can his kingdom stand?

Matthew 13:19: When anyone hears the message about the kingdom and does not understand it, the evil one comes and snatches away what was sown in their heart. This is the seed sown along the path.

Matthew 13:25: But while everyone was sleeping, his enemy came and sowed weeds among the wheat, and went away.

Matthew 13:38–39: The field is the world, and the good seed stands for the people of the kingdom. The weeds are the people of the evil one, and the enemy who sows them is the devil. The harvest is the end of the age, and the harvesters are angels.

Matthew 16:23: Jesus turned and said to Peter, "Get behind me, Satan! You are a stumbling block to me; you do not have in mind the concerns of God, but merely human concerns."

Matthew 17:18: Jesus rebuked the demon, and it came out of the boy, and he was healed at that moment.

Matthew 25:41: Then he will say to those on his left, "Depart from me, you who are cursed, into the eternal fire prepared for the devil and his angels."

Mark 1:23–26: Just then a man in their synagogue who was possessed by an impure spirit cried out, "What do you want with us, Jesus of Nazareth? Have you come to destroy us? I know who you are—the Holy One of God!"

"Be quiet!" said Jesus sternly. "Come out of him!" The impure spirit shook the man violently and came out of him with a shriek.

Mark 1:32–34: That evening after sunset the people brought to Jesus all the sick and demon-possessed. The whole town gathered at the door, and Jesus healed many who had various diseases. He also drove out many demons, but he would not let the demons speak because they knew who he was.

Mark 8:33: But when Jesus turned and looked at his disciples, he rebuked Peter. "Get behind me, Satan!" he said. "You do not have in mind the concerns of God, but merely human concerns."

Mark 9:25: When Jesus saw that a crowd was running to the scene, he rebuked the impure spirit. "You deaf and mute spirit," he said, "I command you, come out of him and never enter him again."

Luke 4:1–13: Jesus, full of the Holy Spirit, left the Jordan and was led by the Spirit into the wilderness, where for forty days he was tempted by the devil. He ate nothing during those days, and at the end of them he was hungry.

The devil said to him, "If you are the Son of God, tell this stone to become bread."

Jesus answered, "It is written: 'Man shall not live on bread alone.'"

The devil led him up to a high place and showed him in an instant all the kingdoms of the world. And he said to him, "I will give you all their authority and splendor; it has been given to me, and I can give it to anyone I want to. If you worship me, it will all be yours."

Jesus answered, "It is written: 'Worship the Lord your God and serve him only.'"

The devil led him to Jerusalem and had him stand on the highest point of the temple. "If you are the Son of God," he said, "throw yourself down from here. For it is written:

"'He will command his angels concerning you
        to guard you carefully;
            they will lift you up in their hands,
    so that you will not strike your foot against a stone.'"

Jesus answered, "It is said: 'Do not put the Lord your God to the test.'"

When the devil had finished all this tempting, he left him until an opportune time.

Luke 11:18: If Satan is divided against himself, how can his kingdom stand? I say this because you claim that I drive out demons by Beelzebub.

Luke 22:31: Simon, Simon, Satan has asked to sift all of you as wheat.

John 8:44: You belong to your father, the devil, and you want to carry out your father's desires. He was a murderer from the beginning, not holding to the truth, for there is no truth in him. When he lies, he speaks his native language, for he is a liar and the father of lies.

John 12:31: Now is the time for judgment on this world; now the prince of this world will be driven out.

John 14:30: I will not say much more to you, for the prince of this world is coming. He has no hold over me.

John 16:8–11: When he comes, he will prove the world to be in the wrong about sin and righteousness and judgment: about sin, because people do not believe in me; about righteousness, because I am going to the Father, where you can see me no longer; and about judgment, because the prince of this world now stands condemned.

Acts 10:38: How God anointed Jesus of Nazareth with the Holy Spirit and power, and how he went around doing good and healing all who were under the power of the devil, because God was with him.

2 Corinthians 4:4: The god of this age has blinded the minds of unbelievers, so that they cannot see the light of the gospel that displays the glory of Christ, who is the image of God.

2 Corinthians 6:15: What harmony is there between Christ and Belial [the prince of evil]? Or what does a believer have in common with an unbeliever?

2 Corinthians 11:3: But I am afraid that just as Eve was deceived by the serpent's cunning, your minds may somehow be led astray from your sincere and pure devotion to Christ.

2 Corinthians 12:7: Or because of these surpassingly great revelations. Therefore, in order to keep me from becoming conceited, I was given a thorn in my flesh, a messenger of Satan, to torment me.

Ephesians 2:2: In which you used to live when you followed the ways of this world and of the ruler of the kingdom of the air, the spirit who is now at work in those who are disobedient.

Ephesians 6:11–12: Put on the full armor of God, so that you can take your stand against the devil's schemes.

For our struggle is not against flesh and blood, but against the rulers, against the authorities, against the powers of this dark world and against the spiritual forces of evil in the heavenly realms.

1 Thessalonians 3:5: For this reason, when I could stand it no longer, I sent to find out about your faith. I was afraid that in some way the tempter had tempted you and that our labors might have been in vain.

2 Thessalonians 2:9–10: The coming of the lawless one will be in accordance with how Satan works. He will use all sorts of displays of power through signs and wonders that serve the lie, and all the ways that wickedness deceives those who are perishing. They perish because they refused to love the truth and so be saved.

1 Timothy 3:6: He must not be a recent convert, or he may become conceited and fall under the same judgment as the devil.

1 Peter 5:8: Be alert and of sober mind. Your enemy the devil prowls around like a roaring lion looking for someone to devour.

1 John 2:13–14: I am writing to you, fathers,
because you know him who is from the beginning.
I am writing to you, young men,
because you have overcome the evil one.
I write to you, dear children,

because you know the Father.
I write to you, fathers,
because you know him who is from the beginning.
I write to you, young men,
because you are strong,
and the word of God lives in you,
and you have overcome the evil one.

1 John 3:8: The one who does what is sinful is of the devil, because the devil has been sinning from the beginning. The reason the Son of God appeared was to destroy the devil's work.

1 John 5:19: We know that we are children of God, and that the whole world is under the control of the evil one.

Revelation 9:11: They had as king over them the angel of the Abyss, whose name in Hebrew is Abaddon and in Greek is Apollyon (that is, Destroyer).

Revelation 12:4: Its tail swept a third of the stars out of the sky and flung them to the earth. The dragon stood in front of the woman who was about to give birth, so that it might devour her child the moment he was born.

Revelation 12:9–10: The great dragon was hurled down—that ancient serpent called the devil, or Satan, who leads the whole world astray. He was hurled to the earth, and his angels with him.

Then I heard a loud voice in heaven say:
"Now have come the salvation and the power
and the kingdom of our God,
and the authority of his Messiah.
For the accuser of our brothers and sisters,
who accuses them before our God day and
night,
has been hurled down."

Revelation 12:12: Therefore rejoice, you heavens
and you who dwell in them!
But woe to the earth and the sea,
because the devil has gone down to you!
He is filled with fury,
because he knows that his time is short.

Revelation 13:4: People worshiped the dragon because he had given authority to the beast, and they also worshiped the beast and asked, "Who is like the beast? Who can wage war against it?"

Revelation 16:14: They are demonic spirits that perform signs, and they go out to the kings of the whole world, to gather them for the battle on the great day of God Almighty.

Revelation 20:10: And the devil, who deceived them, was thrown into the lake of burning sulfur, where the beast and the false prophet had been thrown. They will be tormented day and night for ever and ever.

Bibliography

Bibles

The Holy Bible: King James Version.
The Holy Bible: New International Version. Copyright © 1973, 1978, 1984, 2011 by Biblica Inc.®
The Holy Bible: Revised Standard Version of the Bible, copyright © 1952 (2nd ed., 1971) by the Division of Christian Education of the National Council of the Churches of Christ in the United States of America.
The New American Bible, rev. ed. © 2010, 1991, 1986, 1970. Confraternity of Christian Doctrine, Washington, DC.

Other Works

Alighieri, Dante. *The Divine Comedy: The Inferno, The Purgatorio, and The Paradiso.* Translated by John Ciardi. New York: New American Library, 2003.

Amorth, Gabriele. *An Exorcist Tells His Story.* Translated by Nicoletta V. MacKenzie. San Francisco: Ignatius Press, 1999.

Aquinas, Thomas. *Quaestiones Disputatae de Veritate.* Chicago: Henry Regnery, 1952, 1953, 1954. See https://dhspriory.org/thomas /QDdeVer.htm.

———. *Summa Contra Gentiles.* 5 vols. Notre Dame, IN: University of Notre Dame Press, 1975–97.

———. *Summa Theologiae.* Edited by John Mortensen and Enrique Alarcón. Translated by Laurence Shapcote. Lander, WY: Aquinas Institute for the Study of Sacred Doctrine, 2012.

Aristotle. *Physics.* Translated by Robin Waterfield. New York: Oxford University Press, 2008.

Athenagoras. "A Plea for the Christians (31)." Translated by B. P. Patten. In *Fathers of the Second Century: Hermas, Tatian, Athenagoras, Theophilus, and Clement of Alexandria.* Vol. 2 of *The Ante-Nicene Fathers,* edited by Alexander Roberts, James Donaldson, and Arthur Cleveland Coxe. Reprint, New York: Cosimo Classics, 2007.

Augustine. *The City of God Against the Pagans.* Edited and translated by R. W. Dyson. New York: Cambridge University Press, 1998.

Bellarmine, Robert. *Hell and Its Torments.* Charlotte, NC: Tan Books, 2009.

———. *Spiritual Writings.* Edited and translated by John Patrick Donnelly and Roland J. Teske. New York: Paulist Press, 1989. See chapter 4.

Berger, Peter L. *A Rumor of Angels: Modern Society and the Rediscovery of the Supernatural.* Garden City, NY: Doubleday, 1969.

Bernstein, Alan E. *The Formation of Hell: Death and Retribution in the Ancient and Early Christian Worlds.* Ithaca, NY: Cornell University Press, 1993.

Blanchard, John. *Whatever Happened to Hell?* Wheaton, IL: Crossway, 1995.

Buenting, Joel, ed. *The Problem of Hell: A Philosophical Anthology.* Surrey, UK: Ashgate, 2009.

Camporesi, Piero. *The Fear of Hell: Images of Damnation and Salvation in Early Modern Europe.* Translated by Lucinda Byatt. University Park: Penn State University Press, 1991.

Carson, Donald A. "On Banishing the Lake of Fire." In *The Gagging of God: Christianity Confronts Pluralism.* Grand Rapids, MI: Zondervan, 1996.

Chan, Francis, and Preston Sprinkle. *Erasing Hell: What God Said About Eternity and the Things We've Made Up.* Colorado Springs: David C. Cook, 2011.

Chesterton, G. K. *The Everlasting Man.* Mineola, NY: Dover Publications, 2013.

———. *Orthodoxy.* San Francisco: Ignatius Press, 1995.

———. *St. Francis of Assisi.* New York: Image Books, 1989.

Clement of Rome. "The Second Epistle of Clement (5:5)." In *Fathers of the Third and Fourth Century.* Vol. 7 of *The Ante-Nicene Fathers*, edited by Alexander Roberts, James Donaldson, and Arthur Cleveland Coxe. New York: Cosimo Classics, 2007.

Crockett, William, ed. *Four Views on Hell.* Grand Rapids, MI: Zondervan, 1992.

Cyprian of Carthage. "The Treatises of Cyprian, Treatise V: An Address to Demetrianus." In *Fathers of the Third Century.* Vol. 5 of *The Ante-Nicene Fathers*, edited by Alexander Roberts, James Donaldson, and Arthur Cleveland Coxe. New York: Cosimo Classics, 2007.

Cyril of Jerusalem. "Lecture XVIII (19)." In *Cyril of Jerusalem, Gregory of Nazianzem.* Vol. 7 of *Nicene and Post Nicene Fathers*, 2nd series, edited by Phillip Schaff and Henry Wallace. New York: Cosimo Classics, 2007.

Deak, Esteban. "Apocatastasis: The Problem of Universal Salvation in the Twentieth Century Theology." PhD diss., University of St. Michael's College, 1977.

Denzinger, H., ed. *Enchiridion Symbolorum et Definitionum* (French Edition). Columbia, SC: Wentworth Press, 2018.

DeStefano, Anthony. *Angels All Around Us: A Sightseeing Guide to the Invisible World*. New York: Image, 2011.

———. *Inside the Atheist Mind: Unmasking the Religion of Those Who Say There Is No God*. Nashville, TN: Thomas Nelson, 2018.

———. *Ten Prayers God Always Says Yes To: Divine Answers to Life's Most Difficult Problems*. New York: Doubleday, 2007.

———. *A Travel Guide to Heaven*. New York: Doubleday, 2003.

———. *A Travel Guide to Life: Transforming Yourself from Head to Soul*. New York: FaithWords, 2014.

DiNoia, J. A., Gabriel O'Donnell, Romanus Cessario, and Peter J. Cameron, eds. *The Love That Never Ends: A Key to the Catechism of the Catholic Church*. Huntington, IN: Our Sunday Visitor, 1996.

Dudden, F. Holmes. "The State of Damnation." In *Gregory the Great: His Place in History and Thought*, 2 vols. London: Longmans, Green, and Co., 1905.

Edwards, Jonathan. "Sinners in the Hands of an Angry God." In *Sinners in the Hands of an Angry God and 11 More Classic Messages*. Gainesville, FL: Bridge Logos, 2003.

"Epistle Concerning the Martyrdom of Polycarp (2:3)." In *The Apostolic Fathers with Justin Martyr and Irenaeus*. Vol. 1 of *The Ante-Nicene Fathers*, edited by Alexander Roberts, James Donaldson, and Arthur Cleveland Coxe. New York: Cosimo Classics, 2007.

"The Epistle of Mathetes to Diognetus (10:7)." In *The Apostolic Fathers with Justin Martyr and Irenaeus*. Vol. 1 of *The Ante-Nicene Fathers*, edited by Alexander Roberts, James Donaldson, and Arthur Cleveland Coxe. New York: Cosimo Classics, 2007.

Felix, Minucius. "The Octavius of Minucius Felix (34:12–5:3)." In *Fathers of the Third Century*. Vol. 4 of *The Ante-Nicene Fathers*, edited by Alexander Roberts, James Donaldson, and Arthur Cleveland Coxe. New York: Cosimo Classics, 2007.

Fortin, John R. "Wicked Good: Saint Anselm on the Place of Hell in the Beauty of Creation." *The Saint Anselm Journal* 8, no. 1 (Fall 2012).

Fox, Robert J. *The Catholic Faith*, 262. Huntington, IN: Our Sunday Visitor, 1983.

Garrigou-Lagrange, Reginald. *Life Everlasting and the Immensity of the Soul: A Theological Treatise on the Four Last Things: Death, Judgment, Heaven, Hell*. Charlotte, NC: Tan Books, 1991.

Guillebaud, Harold E. *The Righteous Judge*. N.p.p.: E. Goodman & Son, 1941.

Hilborn, David, ed. *The Nature of Hell*. A Report by the Evangelical Alliance Commission on Unity and Truth Among Evangelicals (ACUTE). Carlisle, UK: Paternoster Press, 2000.

Hippolytus. "Against Plato, On the Cause of the Universe." In *Fathers of the Third* Century. Vol. 5 of *The Ante-Nicene Fathers*, edited by Alexander Roberts, James Donaldson, and Arthur Cleveland Coxe. New York: Cosimo Classics, 2007.

Ignatius. "Epistle of Ignatius to the Ephesians (16:1–2)." In *The Apostolic Fathers with Justin Martyr and Irenaeus*. Vol. 1 of *The Ante-Nicene Fathers*, edited by Alexander Roberts, James Donaldson, and Arthur Cleveland Coxe. New York: Cosimo Classics, 2007.

———. "Irenaeus Against Heresies (1:10:1, 4:28:2)." In *The Apostolic Fathers with Justin Martyr and Irenaeus*. Vol. 1 of *The Ante-Nicene Fathers*, edited by Alexander Roberts, James Donaldson, and Arthur Cleveland Coxe. New York: Cosimo Classics, 2007.

Jones, Brian. *Hell Is Real: But I Hate to Admit It*. Colorado Springs: David C. Cook, 2011.

Jordan, Jeff. "The Topography of Divine Love." *Faith and Philosophy* 29, no. 1 (January 2012): 53–69. https://doi.org/10.5840/faithphil20122913.

Kistler, Don, ed. *The Wrath of Almighty God: Jonathan Edwards on God's Judgment Against Sinners*. Morgan, PA: Soli Deo Gloria, 1996.

Kvanvig, Jonathan L. *The Problem of Hell*. New York: Oxford University Press, 1993.

Lactantius. "Divine Institutes (7:21)." In *Fathers of the Third and Fourth Century*. Vol. 7 of *The Ante-Nicene Fathers*, edited by Alexander Roberts, James Donaldson, and Arthur Cleveland Coxe. New York: Cosimo Classics, 2007.

Lewis, C. S. *The Great Divorce*. New York: HarperOne, 2015.

———. *Mere Christianity*. New York: HarperCollins, 2001.

———. *The Pilgrim's Regress*. Grand Rapids, MI: Eerdmans, 2014.

———. *The Problem of Pain*. New York: HarperOne, 2001.

———. *The Screwtape Letters*. New York: Macmillan, 1982.

Manis, R. Zachary. "Eternity Will Nail Him to Himself: The Logic of Damnation in Kierkegaard's *The Sickness unto Death*." *Religious Studies* 52, no. 3 (September 2016). https://doi.org/10.1017/S0034412515000128.

Martin, Malachi. *Hostage to the Devil*. New York: HarperOne, 2002.

Martin, Regis. *The Last Things: Death, Judgment, Heaven, and Hell*. San Francisco: Ignatius Press, 1998.

Marty, Martin E. "Hell Disappeared. No One Noticed. A Civic Argument." *Harvard Theological Review* 78, nos. 3–4 (October 1985).

Martyr, Justin. "The First Apology of Justin (12, 21, 52)." In *The Apostolic Fathers with Justin Martyr and Irenaeus*. Vol. 1 of *The Ante-Nicene Fathers*, edited by Alexander Roberts, James Donaldson, and Arthur Cleveland Coxe. New York: Cosimo Classics, 2007.

Marthaler, Berard L. "The Second Coming and Judgment." In *The Creed: The Apostolic Faith in Contemporary Theology*. New London, CT: Twenty-Third Publications, 2007.

Matheson, B. "Escaping Heaven." *International Journal of Philosophy of Religion* 75, no. 3 (June 2014): 197–206.

Menezes, Wade L. J. *The Four Last Things: A Catechetical Guide to Death, Judgment, Heaven, and Hell*. Irondale, AL: EWTN Publishing, 2017.

Milton, John. *Paradise Lost*. London, UK: Penguin Books, 1990.

Moore, David George. *The Battle for Hell: A Survey and Evaluation of Evangelicals' Growing Attraction to the Doctrine of Annihilationism*. Lanham, MD: University Press of America, 1995.

Morris, Leon. *The Biblical Doctrine of Judgment.* Eugene, OR: Wipf & Stock, 2006.

Mulder, Jack. *Kierkegaard and the Catholic Tradition.* Bloomington: Indiana University Press, 2010.

Ott, Ludwig. *Fundamentals of Catholic Dogma.* Charlotte, NC: TAN Books, 2009.

Packer, James I. "The Problem of Eternal Punishment." *Evangel: The British Evangelical Review* 10, no. 2 (Summer 1992): 13–19.

Peterson, Robert A. *Hell on Trial: The Case for Eternal Punishment.* Phillipsburg, NJ.: Presbyterian & Reformed Publishing, 1995.

———, and Christopher W. Morgan. *Hell Under Fire: Modern Scholarship Reinvents Eternal Punishment.* Grand Rapids, MI: Zondervan, 2004.

———, and Christopher W. Morgan. *What Is Hell?* Phillipsburg, NJ: Presbyterian & Reformed Publishing , 2010.

Phan, Peter C. *Living into Death, Dying into Life: A Christian Theology of Death and Life Eternal.* Hobe Sound, FL: Lectio Publishing, 2014.

Pieper, Josef. *Death and Immortality.* Translated by Richard and Clara Winston. South Bend, IN: St. Augustine's, 2000.

Pitstick, Alyssa Lyra. *Light in Darkness: Hans Urs Von Balthasar and the Catholic Doctrine of Christ's Descent into Hell.* Grand Rapids, MI: Eerdmans, 2007.

Plantinga, Alvin. *God, Freedom, and Evil.* Grand Rapids, MI: Eerdmans, 1989.

Plutarch. *Plutarch's Moralia,* vol. 7. Translated by Phillip H. de Lacy and Benedict Einardson. Cambridge, MA: Harvard University Press, 1959.

Ratzinger, Joseph. *Eschatology: Death and Eternal Life.* Translated by Michael Waldstein. Washington, DC: Catholic University of America, 1988.

Sartre, Jean-Paule. "No Exit." In *No Exit and The Flies.* New York: Knopf, 1985.

Scupoli, Lorenzo. *The Spiritual Combat.* Manchester, NH: Sophia Press, 2002.

Schwertley, Brian. *The Biblical Doctrine of Hell Examined.* Lansing, MI: Brian Schwertley, 1996. See http://www.reformedonline .com/uploads/1/5/0/3/15030584/the_biblical_doctrine_of_hell _examined.pdf.

Seymour, Charles Steven. *A Theodicy of Hell.* Dordrecht, The Netherlands: Kluwer Academic, 2000.

Sprinkle, Preston, and Stanley N. Gundry, eds. *Four Views on Hell.* 2nd ed. Grand Rapids, MI: Zondervan, 2016.

Sproul, R. C. *Essential Truths of the Christian Faith.* Wheaton, IL: Tyndale House, 1992.

———. *Unseen Realities: Heaven, Hell, Angels and Demons.* Rev. ed. Scotland, UK: Christian Focus, 2011.

Spurgeon, Charles. *Spurgeon on Prayer and Spiritual Warfare.* New Kensington, PA: Whitaker House, 1998.

Sweeney, Jon M. *Inventing Hell: Dante, the Bible, and Eternal Torment.* New York: Jericho Books, 2014.

Swift, Jonathan. *The Place of the Damn'd.* Edited by James D. Woolley. Dublin, Ireland: Trinity Closet Press, 1980.

Swinburne, Richard. "A Theodicy of Heaven and Hell." In *The Existence and Nature of God.* Edited by Alfred J. Freddoso. Notre Dame, IN: University of Notre Dame, 1983.

Tertullian. "Apology (18:3)." Translated by S. Thelwall. In *Latin Christianity.* Vol. 3 of *The Ante-Nicene Fathers*, edited by Alexander Roberts, James Donaldson, and Arthur Cleveland Coxe. New York: Cosimo Classics, 2007.

Theophilus of Antioch. "To Autolycus (1:14)." Translated by Marcus Dods. In *Fathers of the Second Century: Hermas, Tatian, Theophilus, Athenagoras, and Clement of Alexandria.* Vol. 2 of *The Ante-Nicene Fathers*, edited by Alexander Roberts, James Donaldson, and Arthur Cleveland Coxe. New York: Cosimo Classics, 2007.

Toon, Peter. *Heaven and Hell: A Biblical and Theological Overview.* Nashville, TN: Thomas Nelson, 1986.

Turnbull, William B. *The Visions of Tundale.* Victoria, Australia: Leopold Classics Library, 2015.

U.S. Catholic Church. *Catechism of the Catholic Church.* New York: Doubleday, 2003.

Virgil. *The Aeneid.* Translated by Robert Fagles. New York: Penguin Books, 2008.

Von Balthasar, Hans Urs. *Dare We Hope: "That All Men Be Saved"? With a Short Discourse on Hell.* 2nd ed. San Francisco: Ignatius Press, 2014.

Vonier, Anscar. *The Human Soul and Its Relations with Other Spirits.* London: Burns, Oates and Washbourne, 1939.

Vorgrimler, Herbert. *Geschichte der Hölle.* Munich, Germany: W. Fink, 1993.

Youngblood, Ronald F. *Nelson's Illustrated Bible Dictionary.* Nashville, TN: Thomas Nelson, 2014.

Walker, D. P. *The Decline of Hell: Seventeenth-Century Discussions of Eternal Torment.* Chicago: University of Chicago Press, 1964.

Walls, Jerry. *Heaven, Hell, and Purgatory: Rethinking the Things That Matter Most.* Grand Rapids, MI: Brazos Press, 2015.

———. *Hell: The Logic of Damnation.* Notre Dame, IN: University of Notre Dame Press, 1992.

———. ed. *The Oxford Handbook of Eschatology.* New York: Oxford University Press, 2008.

Wiersbe, Warren W. *The Strategy of Satan.* Carol Stream, IL: Tyndale House, 1979.

Notes

AN INFERNAL ITINERARY

1. Revelation 19:20; 20:10; 20:14–15; 21:18; 20:14; 21:8; Matthew 8:12; Luke 13:28.
2. Matthew 5:22, 29–30, 10:28, 18:19, 23:15, 33; Mark 9:43, 45, 47; Luke 12:5.
3. Isaiah 66:23; Matthew 25:31–46; John 5:28–29; 1 Corinthians 15:51–52; 2 Corinthians 5:10; Revelation 20:12.

CHAPTER 1: THE STARTING POINT OF OUR TRIP

1. Genesis 4.
2. R. J. Rummel, *Death by Government* (New Brunswick, NJ: Transaction Publishers, 1994), 77, 141, 363.
3. Jeremiah 17:9; Matthew 15:19; Luke 6:45; John 3:19; Romans 2:1–29, 7:14–25, 7:21.
4. Matthew 15:16–20, 23:1–12; Mark 7:14–23, 12:38–40; Luke 11:37–54, 20:45–47.

CHAPTER 2: THE ORIGIN OF HELL

1. Genesis 1–2.
2. Deuteronomy 33:2; Psalms 68:7, 17; 1 Samuel 17:45;
   2 Chronicles 18:18; Nehemiah 9:6; Jeremiah 33:22; Daniel
   7:9–10; 2 Kings 6:11–17; Matthew 26:53; Romans 9:29; James
   5:4; Hebrews 12:18–24; Revelation 5:11–12.
3. Genesis 3:24; Isaiah 6:2; Psalms 122:5; Colossians 1:16;
   Ephesians 3:10; 1 Thessalonians 4:16; Jude 9; Revelation 5:11.
4. Psalms 104:4; Mark 12:25.
5. Luke 20:36.
6. Genesis 3:24, 19:15, 22:11; Judges 13:19–21; Luke 17:29; Acts
   12:7; Revelation 8–9, 15–16; 2 Peter 2:11.
7. Revelation 12:7.
8. Isaiah 14:12.
9. Isaiah 14:13–14.
10. Revelation 12:7–9; Jude 9.
11. Revelation 12:4.
12. Matthew 24:36.
13. John 8:44.
14. John 8:12, 9:5; 1 John 1:5; Luke 10:18.
15. Psalm 8; Revelation 20.

CHAPTER 3: HALFWAY TO HELL

1. Ecclesiastes 12:7.
2. 1 Corinthians 14:14; Romans 8:16; Luke 23:43; Acts 7:59;
   Philippians 1:23–24; 2 Corinthians 5:8; Revelation 6:9–10.
3. 1 Kings 17:19–23; Ecclesiastes 12:5–7; Matthew 17:1–3, 22:31–
   32; Luke 16:19–31, 23:39–43.
4. 2 Corinthians 12:8–9; Romans 1:5; Acts 6:8, 15:11; Ephesians
   2:8, 4:7, 4:16; Hebrews 13:9.
5. John 3:19–20.
6. Hebrews 9:27.
7. Matthew 22:30; Mark 12:25.

8. C. S. Lewis, *Mere Christianity* (San Francisco: HarperSanFrancisco, 2001), 94.
9. 2 Peter 3:9; Acts 11:18.
10. Matthew 12:31.

CHAPTER 4: FALLING LIKE LIGHTNING

1. 1 Timothy 2:4; 2 Peter 3:9; Ezekiel 18:23; Matthew 23:37.
2. Colossians 1:16–17; Hebrews 1:3, 4:13; Psalm 24:1–2, 29:10, 147:5; Matthew 19:26.
3. Gilbert Keith Chesterton, Quotes [website], https://www.quotes.net/quote/11797.
4. Luke 16:19–31.
5. Luke 23:33–43.
6. Ecclesiastes 11:9, 12:14; Hebrews 9:27; 2 Corinthians 5.
7. Joel 3:14; Ezekiel 13:5; Isaiah 2:12; Matthew 24:27, 25:31; John 6:39–40; Acts 10:42, 17:31; Romans 2:5–16, 14:10; 1 Corinthians 4:5; 2 Corinthians 5:10; 2 Timothy 4:1; 2 Thessalonians 1:5; James 5:7.
8. Genesis 2:7; Wisdom 2:22–23; Ecclesiastes 12:7; Proverbs 15:24; Isaiah 35:10, 51:6; Daniel 12:2.
9. 1 John 1:5; Psalms 36:9; John 1:9; Revelation 21:23.
10. Matthew 22:32; Luke 16:23; 1 Corinthians 15; Revelation 2:17.
11. Romans 2:15–16.
12. Isaiah 14:12.
13. Luke 10:18.
14. Isaiah 48:22.

CHAPTER 5: AVOIDING A WRONG TURN

1. Isaiah 66:24; Mark 9:48.
2. Genesis 1:27.
3. Genesis 2:7.
4. 1 Corinthians 13:12; Matthew 4:23.
5. See the appendix.

6. Genesis 1:1, 27; Psalm 104:24; Exodus 31:1–6, 35:31–32; Romans 12:6; Hebrews 2:4.

CHAPTER 6: A PREVIEW OF PAIN

1. Jeremiah 2:13; Matthew 22:13.
2. 1 Corinthians 13:12.
3. 1 Corinthians 13:8–13; Matthew 18:10; 1 John 3:2; 2 Corinthians 5:6–8.
4. Psalm 16:2; Matthew 19:17; James 1:17.
5. Genesis 1:27; Psalm 27:4, 50:1–2; John 14:16, 18:37.
6. 1 John 4:7–21.
7. Matthew 11:28–30; John 14:27; 2 Thessalonians 3:16; Philippians 4:7.

CHAPTER 7: ARRIVAL IN HELL

1. Matthew 24:36.
2. Aristotle, *Physics*, bk. 4, trans. Robin Waterfield (Oxford: Oxford University Press, 1999), 111.
3. 2 Peter 3:8.
4. 1 Corinthians 3:13; Ecclesiastes 12:14; Matthew 12:36; Romans 2:16.
5. Romans 14:11; Isaiah 45:23.
6. Charles Haddon Spurgeon, "Jesus, the Judge," The Spurgeon Center, May 25, 1879, https://www.spurgeon.org /resource-library/sermons/jesus-the-judge#flipbook/.
7. 1 Corinthians 13:12; Luke 8:17; 1 John 3:2.
8. Acts 10:42, 17:31; John 5:22; Romans 2:5–6; 1 Corinthians 4:5; 2 Corinthians 5:10; Isaiah 66:15–24; Matthew 12:36–37, 25:31–46; Revelation 20:11–12.
9. Luke 12:2–3.
10. John 16:23.
11. Reginald Garrigou-Lagrange, *Life Everlasting and the Immensity of the Soul: A Theological Treatise on the Four Last Things: Death,*

Judgment, Heaven, Hell (Charlotte, NC: Tan Books, 1991), 74–75.

12. Revelation 20:12–13; Isaiah 30:18, 61:8.

13. Isaiah 66:23.

14. John 5:28–29 esv.

15. Luke 20:37–38.

16. Matthew 25:31–33, 46 esv.

17. 1 Corinthians 15:51–52.

18. 2 Corinthians 5:10.

19. Revelation 20:12.

20. 1 Corinthians 15:20.

21. Matthew 26:41.

22. Matthew 13:12.

CHAPTER 8: A MONSTROUS MAKEOVER

1. 1 Corinthians 15:42, 52–54.

2. Mark 9:48 nasb.

3. Isaiah 66:24.

4. John 9:2–3.

5. 1 Corinthians 6:19.

6. 1 Corinthians 15:44–45.

7. 1 Corinthians 15:20–23, 42–53.

8. Matthew 23:27.

9. Revelation 20:12.

10. Matthew 10:15.

11. Luke 10:13–14.

12. Revelation 18:7.

13. 1 Corinthians 15:20.

14. Acts 24:15; John 5:28–29; Matthew 25:31–32, 46.

CHAPTER 9: EXPLORING THE TERRAIN

1. Genesis 1:31.

2. Revelation 9:1–3, 20:3; Luke 8:31.

3. Revelation 21:1.
4. Matthew 13:12.
5. Matthew 8:12, 13:42, 18:8–9, 22:13, 25:30; Mark 9:48; Revelation 14:10–11, 20:10, 15; Jude 13.
6. C. S. Lewis, *The Screwtape Letters*, rev. ed. (New York: Macmillan, 1982), 103.
7. Job 15:21.
8. Isaiah 34:3.
9. See the appendix.
10. Jude 6; 2 Peter 2:4; Revelation 20:2.
11. R. C. Sproul, *Essential Truths of the Christian Faith* (Wheaton, IL: Tyndale House, 1992), 286.

CHAPTER 10: ACTIVITIES IN HELL: PART I
1. Revelation 9:1–12.
2. Job 4:15.
3. 1 Corinthians 13:4–7; Luke 22:19.
4. John 8:34.
5. John 8:32.
6. 2 Peter 2:11.
7. Jeremiah 2:20.
8. John Milton, *Paradise Lost*, bk. 1, line 263.
9. Isaiah 14:12–15; Job 41:34.
10. Luke 22:31; Job 1–2; Revelation 12:10.
11. Luke 4:18 ESV.

CHAPTER 11: ACTIVITIES IN HELL: PART II
1. Psalm 37:28, 86:5; Romans 12:19; Isaiah 61:8–9; Luke 6:36; Ephesians 2:4; Titus 3:5.
2. Psalm 62:12 KJV.
3. Romans 2:6.
4. Hebrews 10:29.
5. Matthew 25:41–46.
6. Matthew 7:7–8.

7. Romans 2:6.
8. C. S. Lewis, *The Screwtape Letters*, rev. ed. (New York: Macmillan, 1982), 41–42.
9. Luke 16:19–31.
10. Dante Alighieri, *The Divine Comedy*, trans. John Ciardi (New York: Penguin Books, 2003), 54.
11. Philippians 4:7.

CHAPTER 12: ACTIVITIES IN HELL: PART III
1. Revelation 21:8.
2. Matthew 20:26–28; John 15:13; Philippians 3:10–11.
3. Acts 17:28.
4. See Edward Fudge, *The Fire That Consumes: A Biblical and Historical Study of the Doctrine of Final Punishment*, 3rd ed. (Eugene, OR: Cascade Books, 2011), or Philip Edgcumbe Hughes, *The True Image: The Origin and Destiny of Man in Christ* (Grand Rapids, MI: Eerdmans, 1989).

CHAPTER 13: A DAY IN HELL
1. Matthew 25:46.
2. Matthew 18:8.
3. Mark 9:48.
4. Mark 9:48.
5. 2 Thessalonians 1:8 ESV.
6. Jude 6.
7. Jude 7.
8. Jude 13 KJV.
9. Revelation 14:11, 19:3.
10. Revelation 20:10 KJV.
11. C. S. Lewis, *The Problem of Pain* (San Francisco: HarperSanFrancisco, 2001), 126.
12. Mark 3:29.
13. John 8:58.
14. Revelation 8:1, 22:2.

CHAPTER 14: HELL ON EARTH

1. Matthew 3:2 ESV.
2. Romans 1:5, 16:26 ESV.
3. Colossians 1:27.
4. Philippians 4:7.
5. 1 Peter 5:8; 2 Timothy 2:26.
6. Revelation 1:8; Exodus 3:14; Romans 1:20; Psalm 102:27; Malachi 3:6; James 1:17.
7. 1 Peter 5:8.
8. See the appendix.
9. Acts 16:18.
10. Ephesians 6:12.
11. Genesis 3.
12. Matthew 4:17; Luke 13:3; Acts 3:19; Romans 2:5, 5:21, 8:3; Isaiah 55:7.
13. 1 Peter 1:18–20; 2 Corinthians 5:21; Philippians 2:7.
14. John 8:44.
15. John 10:10, 14:6; Matthew 28:19.
16. Anthony DeStefano, *Inside the Atheist Mind: Unmasking the Religion of Those Who Say There Is No God* (Nashville, TN: Thomas Nelson, 2018), 99–105, 108–113.
17. 1 Corinthians 14:33.

CHAPTER 15: TICKET TO HELL?

1. 1 Timothy 2:4; 2 Peter 3:9.
2. Matthew 12:31; Mark 3:29; Luke 12:10.
3. Isaiah 1:18.
4. Romeo Hontiveros, "The Sacrament of Confession by Archbishop Fulton Sheen," PagadianDiocese.org, May 17, 2014, http://www.pagadiandiocese.org/2014/05/17/the-sacrament-of-confession-by-archbishop-fulton-sheen/.
5. Numbers 23:19; Hebrews 6:18; Titus 1:2.
6. Romans 6:23.
7. 1 Corinthians 15:32.

8. Ephesians 6:10–20; Matthew 28:19; Micah 6:8; James 1:27.

9. James 4:10; Luke 14:11; Proverbs 11:2; Psalm 149:4; Acts 3:19.

10. James 4:7.

11. Philippians 2:11; 1 Corinthians 15:57; John 10:9, 14:6.

12. 1 Corinthians 2:9 KJV.

13. Revelation 7:16–17, 21:4–7, 22:1–5; Psalm 36:5–9; 2 Peter 3:13; John 14:1–3, 3:16.

About the Author

Anthony DeStefano is the bestselling author of more than twenty Christian books for adults and children. He has appeared on many national television and radio programs, including *Fox and Friends*, *Huckabee*, *EWTN Live*, and *The 700 Club*. His author website is: www.AnthonyDeStefano.com.